The Love Disorder

by

Conrad Boeding, M.A.
with
Ed McManis

© 1998 by Conrad Boeding, M.A.
All rights reserved. No part of this publication may be reproduced in any form without written permission from Passages Press, 777 S. Wadsworth Blvd., Bldg. 1, Suite 105, Lakewood, CO 80226. Phone: (303) 914-9729 • Fax: (303) 914-9733
e-mail: hpi@creek.net

Printed in the United States of America

To Erin, Lisa, Megan, and Amanda—my children, who continually fill my heart with an abundance of love.

Table of Contents

Forward vii
Acknowledgements ix
About the Author xi
Introduction xii
Prologue: Important "Stuff" xviii
My Little Glass Doll xxi

Section One:	**Looking For Love In All the Wrong Places** 1	
Chapter 1:	Modern Living: A Game The Whole Family Can Play…But Doesn't 2	
Chapter 2:	"Because I said so, that's why!" 7	
Chapter 3:	The Shrinking Safety Zone 11	
	Bang! Bang! You're Next 13	
	Turn On, Tune In, Drop Dead 16	
	Sex is Not a Four-Letter Word 17	
Chapter 4:	Aliens on a Small Planet 21	
Section Two:	**Love Is A Many Splendored Thing…If** 27	
Chapter 5:	The Ties That Should Bind 28	
Chapter 6:	Those Crucial First Two Years 33	
Chapter 7:	The "Moreso" Theory (Filling in the Blueprint) 37	
Chapter 8:	A "Security" Deposit 41	

Section Three:	**(Everything I Do) I Do It For You** 49
Chapter 9:	What About DAT? 50
Chapter 10:	Partnership: The Special Glue 63
	Every Human Core 64
	Distancing Human Qualities 67
	The Layers of the Defense Structure 73
Chapter 11:	The Partnership Model of Discipline 83
Section Four:	**The More I Know You...The More I Love You** 85
Chapter 12:	Prerequisites for Effective Partnering in Discipline 86
	About You 87
	About the Child 87
	Fear/Rage 89
	Sadness/Loss 89
	Loss of Trust 90
	Need to Self-Parent 90
	Reversed Behavior Patterns 90
	About the Disturbance (Diagnosis) 91
Chapter 13:	Variations on a Theme 95
	Secure Attachment 95
	Ricky 96
	Attachment Disorders 101
	Anxious Attachment 102
	Michelle 104
	Avoidant Attachment 113
	A.J. 114
	Ambivalent Attachment 121
	Kerry 123

v

Section Five:	**Love Is Lovelier The Second Time Around**	131
Chapter 14:	Attachment Principles	132
	Create the Velvet Box	133
	Work in Partnership	134
	Recreate the Attachment Cycle Whenever Possible	136
	Work With What They Give You	139
	It's All About Distance	143
	Their World Stops When...	146
	Using Control to Nurture	146
Chapter 15:	Tools to Implement the Attachment Principles	149
	Provide the Tools	149
	Teach the Tools of Discipline	154
	Create Gifts to Accompany the Tools of Discipline	157
Epilogue		157
References		161

Foreward

As co-founders of Wellspring Foundation, we have engaged in the residential treatment of severely emotionally disturbed adolescents for more than 20 years. This is difficult and demanding work: deeply satisfying, sometimes exhilarating, but always sorrowful in the pain and struggle of these wounded children and their parents who, for the most part, have tried to do the best they could with what they, themselves, have been given.

We are grateful that Conrad Boeding has put this important work on parenting and attachment therapy in writing. As colleague and compatriot in this common effort, we know Connie as a man who is deeply committed through his love and compassion for children and parents. He is a superb therapist and trainer, a former teacher and coach with a great heart and delightful sense of humor. He inspires immediate confidence in the young people and parents with whom he works. They know instinctively that he can be trusted – that he will respect them, coach them, and keep them safe even in the throes of their deepest vulnerability. They are relieved by the sheer size of this intelligent, artful, gentle giant. He could, after all, protect them from the violence inside they most fear.

There are techniques and techniques, and, from personal experience, Dynamic Attachment Therapy is very effective in creating breakthroughs where love and trust have broken down or have never been established. It offers the consistently secure environment that is so necessary for working through emotions of pain and anger and terror that, predictably, become walls between child and parent – and, if left untended, between child and the world.

At Wellspring, we are under the constant press of managed care, and DAT has provided ways to treat children and families with severe attachment difficulties successfully within short residential stays and outpatient treatment.

Connie's methods work, *and* they can be taught. He presents his partnership model of discipline and the principles and process of DAT in a clear, incisive manner, deftly and with humor. What you will find in these pages is a practical guidebook for parents and professionals traversing a most difficult passage. What cannot be taught, but only modeled, is Connie's artistry, his integrity, and his own God-given gifts as a healer – the deep spirituality that resonates through the love, compassion, and no-nonsense discipline of his methodology.

At stake in this endeavor is trust in love itself and in its ultimate victory over desperate measures taken in order to wield power and control over others and – all too often – the violence they engender. Non-attachment erodes conscience and turns loveless children into murderers; *something* must happen to reverse this trend. Given the state of our society, the need for sound and sophisticated interventions has never been greater. DAT is such an intervention. Thankfully, Conrad Boeding, its author and mediator, has become a significant force in the responsible development of attachment therapy as a medium to address levels of disorder that more traditional methods of therapy have been unable to reach.

Phyllis and Richard Beauvais
Co-founders
Wellspring Foundation
Bethlehem, CT

Acknowledgements

I wish to thank the many people who have directly influenced the thinking and actual compilation of this book. First, there is the great Dr. Foster Cline, who helped me launch my career in 1983. His guidance and wisdom provided the basis of my curiosity for attachment dynamics. I also owe a great deal of thanks to Bob and Kathy Lay — foster parents extraordinaire – for teaching me how to implement attachment principles in the trenches.

A major influence was my wonderful doctoral internship in 1986 at Forest Heights Lodge in Evergreen, Colorado, with Russ Colburn, Vera Fahlberg, and Ray Curtis as my mentors. Their perspectives gave the insight that was to become the basis for the Dynamic Attachment Therapy we have developed at Human Passages.

When I founded Human Passages Institute (HPI) in 1991, I had some valuable collaboration with my staff. Thank you to Randy Stanko, Bill Exline, David Hollingsworth, and John Welch – and, of course, my dedicated assistant, Wanda Beck. And, as HPI grew and transitioned (moved to Lakewood, CO in 1994), so did the incredible attachment work (DAT) we were doing with families throughout the country and Canada – as well as the development of our therapeutic foster program here at home in Colorado. The lion's share of that load was carried by Carole McKelvey and Lisa Aldrich. HPI would literally not be here today if it weren't for those two wonderful people.

That brings us to today's HPI staff, who are like family in their singular focus of helping children and families within the DAT model. Lisa, Bob, Diane, Kate, Chris,

Mandy, Terol, and Cindy – your commitment, competence, and passion amaze me. A very special thank you goes to HPI Clinical Director Diane Fineberg, who contributed significant time, energy, and ideas to this book.

As for the book itself, Ed, you make it look easy. Thank you, Ed McManis, for your tenacity, style, ideas, enthusiasm and expertise in helping get these thoughts in writing. Thank you, my friends, Richard and Phyllis Beauvais, founders of Wellspring in Bethlehem, CT, for writing the forward. You have the most incredible residential treatment facility imaginable.

And thank you, Kim Thomas, for your many hours of design and layout (without whining) and for your desktop publishing expertise. Thank you even more for your humor, support, great suggestions – including the idea for the title of this book and excellent quote from your Master's Paper on Attachment Disorder and Attachment Therapy – and for introducing me to the editor I didn't even know I needed. Finally, thank you to Judith Champion, who really *is* one. Thank you for editing this book. Your heart-felt care and enthusiasm for developing, promoting, and communicating the essence of our attachment work has really made a positive difference. Most of all, thank you for "hanging in there" with me and helping me find the best words to convey the message of my life-work.

About the Author

Conrad Boeding grew up in Denver, earned his Bachelor of Arts degree at Regis College (now University), with double majors (psychology and philosophy) and double minors (sociology and theology). He received his Masters from the University of Northern Colorado in education with an emphasis in psychology. He has also completed further graduate work toward a doctorate in professional psychology at the University of Denver.

Connie founded Human Passages Institute in 1991. He lives in the foothills west of Denver; if he has any spare time, he enjoys playing the guitar and participates in numerous team and individual sporting activities. He has four grown children.

He says he is on the journey, too: living life, trying to get it right. He continues developing himself and his contribution, which is to leave a legacy that helps others find and further their purpose.

Introduction

This book is a treasure. The secrets it reveals have been buried deep inside someone you love or care about: a lonely or belligerent child, an angry teen, an "invisible" or withdrawn adult. If you have been seeking the cache of its riches, you may have given up long ago, grudgingly resigned that you would never find the answers – if, indeed, any answers ever existed to begin with.

They do. If there is someone you just can't reach – someone whose behavior defies explanation – and you feel desperate to begin to grasp the why and wherefore, take a deep breath and dive in here. The explanation for every specific question you have may not lie within these pages, but if you're hungry for some good, solid understanding about the seemingly unfathomable circumstances that brought you here to this moment and all its attendant confusion, read on. This is fertile ground. Your search is likely to be fruitful.

Why "The Love Disorder"?

Because the kids this book is written about are unable to give and receive love. It is that simple and that complex. Something has happened that has rendered them unable to accept what you and others have to offer and equally incapable of giving it back.

The first component of this phrase, "love," has many connotations – maybe too many. We use it to describe how we feel about pizza or chocolate eclairs, comfortable shoes or the birthday gift Aunt Shirley sent, the tingling attraction we feel for someone we have a crush on or the earthy smell that precedes a thunderstorm. In many cases, "love" is used to mean "I like this a lot."

We're speaking of its more mystical meaning – that impossible-to-define link that happens among and between people who genuinely care for each other and is composed of esteem, respect, affection, admiration, approval, and sometimes certain levels of adoration and devotion.

Whatever it is, it is necessary to our ability to thrive as fully human beings. As our friend and colleague Kim Thomas wrote in one of her graduate papers about attachment:

> Learning to love is vital. It is the most fundamental goal of human life. Our most basic experience is relationship. Our greatest teacher is relationship. Our deepest fears are created because of relationship. Our greatest longing is for relationship. Our deepest and most mysterious emotion is based in relationship. It is love.[1]

A child is like a container of needs (see Figure 5 on page 52 for reference). When an infant's most basic needs – including food, touch, movement, comfort and safety – are not consistently fulfilled, trust disintegrates (or is prevented from forming at all), and the ability to learn to love is interrupted and impaired.

There are practical differences between instinct, bonding, and attachment, and these are discussed in Chapter 5. One early specialist in this field saw attachment as being "akin to...learning to give and receive love..." That premise has been largely – if not universally – accepted by the attachment therapy community, so it stands to reason that interrupting the formation of healthy attachments also adversely affects the ability to give and receive love. This theme is revisited several times throughout this book, including Chapter 9.

One of the saddest commentaries on contemporary society is that far too few children have the experience of knowing and experiencing love in their lives. That brings us to the "disorder" part of the title.

In traditional medical or clinical terms, a "disorder" refers to some kind of malady – an illness or disease, an ailment or complaint. It is a convenient catch-all way of saying that some body part or mental component isn't present or doesn't function properly. In other words, something that should be there is missing or doesn't work – which keeps the whole behavioral system from working correctly. In the psychotherapy community, a particular set of symptoms – often unpleasant – and behaviors is given a name, and the word "disorder" is added to it to give it credibility. It then becomes an accepted label in the language of diagnosis, the "peg-hole" that serves to somehow "define" kids who are unmanageable or whose behavior we don't understand.

Our usage of the word follows this thinking only in part. The presenters of this book agree that something significant is out of whack and needs specialized attention. However, we believe that the insides of children who are so vehemently defended against love more closely resemble some of the alternate definitions of the word "disorder"; when it comes to loving and being loved, their experiences are more like bedlam, chaos, commotion, turmoil, uproar, mayhem, confusion, disarray. In other words, a whole lot more is in the mix than there should be in terms of sheer "inner noise."

Who could live productively with this kind of primary reality? To not feel love is to not feel the essence of life itself – and they know they're missing out. That's why they're angry and despairing. Love isn't supposed to be terrifying.

(One important distinction here is the difference between someone feeling unloved or not being able to feel love in the first place. These kids literally can't let themselves feel. In this case, we are talking about individuals to whom allowing real feelings inside themselves is tantamount to threatening them with utter annihilation. This is addressed in much greater detail inside.)

Is it any wonder that kids who can't even feel love to begin with – even if it's consistently being showered all over them with great sincerity and enthusiasm – are filled with rage and bitterness about this most colossal rip-off of all? Viewed from this perspective, perhaps we can all begin to understand (not condone) and feel some compassion for the behavior they exhibit.

This isn't their fault. It's not your fault, either, even if you are parenting a child who is having severe behavioral problems. These kids aren't simply being randomly uncooperative – there's been some real damage done that must be recognized, suitably acknowledged, and patiently repaired. You can gain a lot of valuable information and insights from reading this book that you couldn't have been expected to know otherwise.

This is important. In reality, there is no blame, and there is no guilt. This book is about taking whatever responsibility you can, to use your abilities and talents and time and energy and resources to make sure that your child gets the help she needs. It is also about teaching her that she is responsible for her own actions and that she is accountable for the ways she behaves.

Neither you nor your child have failed. You've just been incomplete in your understanding – much the same way she has been incomplete in her ability to form and trust healthy attachments. Now that you are about to learn about the processes that cause disruption, focus on using this knowledge to encourage healing and wholeness. Get involved by learning how to be an effective adult partner (Chapter 11) for a child or teen who needs you.

We also want to remind you that these kids are bright, original, and extraordinarily creative. They have to be in order to survive the chaotic contradictions of their lives. They just haven't learned to get it all lined up in ways that work to their highest advantage yet. The best news is that they can learn, they can be taught.

As alluded to a moment ago, the diagnoses of many children center around the symptoms they present, because many mental health assessments are not designed to look behind the appearances in order to find out the causes of the actions. These demonstrations of maladaptive behavior are actually windows into the turmoil that boils inside these kids – if the diagnosing therapist has the trained eyes and ears and open heart to recognize incomplete attachment formation.

As such, this book may be of special interest to those who have or are in regular contact with kids who have been diagnosed with Attention Deficit Disorder, Conduct Disorder, Oppositional Defiant Disorder, etc. Statistically, a strong possibility exists that beneath the presenting behaviors is a history of disruption of healthy attachment formation.

While no "magic potion" can be offered, the process of finding out that there are tried and tested methods of dealing with kids who live with these difficulties may be a revelation that changes your life and gives you hope. It is possible to teach children – and even grown-ups – who have experienced attachment disruptions to re-attach and accept – or even seek out – love and guidance and discipline from supportive adults. They can learn to be accountable for their behaviors, to accept responsibility for themselves, and to live lives of value and integrity. Although no therapeutic approach offers guarantees, the success rates for clients of Dynamic Attachment Therapy have been encouraging.

What follows are a few particulars about the way this book is written.

The clients included in the narrative are real, genuine human beings and not composites of case studies. Their names have, of course, been changed to protect their privacy.

In order to be as inclusive as possible and also to avoid any gender-bias, we have attempted to alternate the use of male and female pronouns throughout the text.

Statements or opinions not referenced by footnotes or attributed to others are those of the author.

All section headings are named after songs (or are borrowed from song titles), perhaps (I'm speculating) because you are being subliminally invited to dance...

...So, if you've been on a "treasure hunt" for help with someone who has seemed impossible to reach, prepare to dive deep into this guidebook to the inner reaches of what has mostly been, until now, a secret world. You may be able to illumine a lonely life with your newfound understanding. As a bonus, one of the faces that begins to clear and relax from receiving the benefits of your new perceptions and compassion just may be your own.

Judith Champion
Boulder, Colorado
October 1998

Prologue

Important "Stuff"

Several years ago, Donald graduated from high school, and, like the thousands of other seniors who marched down the aisle in cap and gown – while their families snapped pictures – he clutched his diploma, hopeful for his future.

But for this bright young man, graduation marked a triumph over a history of problems. At 18, he could just as easily have been marching to jail, handcuffed, his mugshot the only picture snapped.

When I first met Donald, he was 14 and in trouble. Three months previously, while in the P.E. locker room at school, he had wrapped a chain around another student's neck and tried to choke him. In my first session with Donald, I asked him why. He looked at me, shrugged, and said, "He got into my stuff."

How valuable was Donald's stuff? A pair of shorts, some socks, a pocketful of change; yet, his 14-year-old values system told him his "stuff" equaled another person's life. Donald knew no alternative response.

Fortunately, during the next two years, with hard work and help from his family, Donald began to gain a more realistic perception of the importance of "stuff."

In my work, I see hundreds of kids like Donald struggling in a world where "stuff" is often more valued than people. "Kids at risk," we call them. Alternative Youth.

(Alternative to what?) Some, like Donald, find their way through adolescence, graduate, move on to have fulfilling lives with solid relationships. Others never make it to the graduation podium. They become the teenage statistics in the "Summer of Violence," the kid in the drive-by shooting, the runaway girl, the broken adoption and multiple placements for the kid in the foster care system, the high school dropout with "so much potential" who gets arrested for burglary or prostitution.

We professionals – psychologists, social workers, therapists, teachers – have done a thorough job of identifying and labeling the problem kids: they are unattached, oppositional, defiant, conduct-disordered, attention deficit disordered, bi-polar disordered, hyperactive, depressed. Still, the statistics mount, and the damage is done. The problems teenagers face seem more complicated and dangerous each year, and rarely do we hear enough about the success stories.

When I first started teaching high school, I knew I had a calling to hear and understand kids. Throughout 20 years of teaching, coaching, and raising my own four children, I learned about kids. I learned to use the classroom atmosphere, or the basketball court, or a simple one-to-one opportunity to help them make better choices, to get through. I knew the primary value of my job wasn't necessarily about the content of the activity – but, rather, the process of relating and developing a bond with the student. I always wanted to show the kids, especially the "misfits," that there was someone on the other side of the desk: an adult who could hear them and not betray them.

I also learned about the balance kids need: confrontation and challenge, but also compassion and concern. I learned, too, what wasn't successful – too much confrontation got results, but also resentment; too much nurturing didn't provide enough structure. Too much mercy left little room for justice.

Most importantly, I've learned that every kid has a good core underneath. I've never met a purely unattached kid. When I tell this to other professionals or therapists, they usually give me a sideways glance and smile. "You've never met Johnny," they say.

Still, I believe every child can be reached. When I assess a child, I have to ask, "What made this person have to cover her heart, her core? Does this child have a value system? Show remorse? Does she have a conscience?"

This book is about kids like Donald – kids who can neither give love nor let love in – pre-adolescents and teenagers who have covered their cores with at-risk behaviors: acting out, drug and alcohol abuse, running away. Sometimes the problem is as simple as, "I want Mom and Dad to spend more time with me." Sometimes the problem is multi-faceted: there is a physiological disturbance as well as an emotional disruption. Regardless, both children are on the same spectrum. It's a question of degree, not kind.

Too often, we divide our kids into "good" ones and "bad" ones, the healthy and the crazy. My work has proven to me that each one of us and our children has a core that needs protecting. The fact is that some of us are more or less at risk of using dangerous and defeating behaviors.

Finally, this book is about reaching and healing kids. It's about the kids who are protecting their "stuff" because they can't trust anyone. It's about the struggle to reach more kids like Donald – and what will happen if we don't.

My Little Glass Doll

I have this glass doll.
She goes to sleep with me at night.
She dances in my dreams.
She is happy and it makes me happy.
She laughs and I laugh with her.
It's like she's inside of me, protecting me.
She wakes up with me and the nightmare begins.
The world is such a scary, dark place,
    But my little glass doll is my only friend.
I carry my body through the road of the world,
    But I am not alone.
My little glass doll follows me.
The world is against me and intends to hurt me.
The world is fooled by me.
I fight the world and my little glass doll helps me.
Sometimes I hate my little glass doll,
    Because she helps me fool the world.
I want the world to love me.
    But she won't let me love the world.
That's okay.
    Oh well, at least she won't let anyone hurt me.
I'm fooling you
    Because that little glass doll is me.

April 8, 1997
18-year-old therapy client, Human Passages Institute.

Section One
Looking For Love In All The Wrong Places

That's exactly what kids with the Love Disorder do to fill their yearning to be in loving, caring relationships. Because of the pain and loss that result from their mistrust of and alienation from the adult caregivers in their lives, they become incredibly defended. They remain empty and alienated – unable to take in the love and values historically offered within the family context. But, because nothing can live in a vacuum, they are driven to "fill up" with something – anything that will postpone their pain and emptiness from not being able to love or be loved. They often become risk-takers with sex, drugs, and rock 'n' roll, wanting the excitement that living on the edge brings them. From their perspective, they are "just having fun;" simply "hanging out with their friends;" and "getting out of this boring house" – "whatever." From our perspective, they are indifferent to our guidance; out of control with their bad attitudes and high-risk behavior, and worst of all, "looking for love in all the wrong places."

Chapter 1

Modern Living: A Game The Whole Family Can Play...But Doesn't

In his book *Slapstick*,[1] Kurt Vonnegut, the noted American satirist, introduces us to the notion of the extended family: it's not just grandparents, cousins, nephews – but a global family where each individual is assigned by number to a family of thousands.

Just as the African proverb suggests that it takes an entire village to raise a child, Vonnegut expands that notion by saying that, in today's culture, it takes a *world* to raise a child. From that perspective, what chance does the fragile triad of Mom, Dad, and child have when sailing their family lifeboat on the stormy seas of modern society? But with relatives scattered throughout the United States and around the globe, the family can at least find refuge through their connections in many ports and have a better chance.

Although Vonnegut's notion is more pointed satire than practical solution, the concept is valid, nonetheless. First Lady Hillary Rodham Clinton's book, *It Takes A Village*,[2] brought this concept of family back to center stage in the U.S. All politics aside, I think everyone would support the notion that nothing is more important, sacred, or fragile than the family. And in today's world, where even the *definition* of family cannot be agreed upon – nuclear, single-parent, same-sex parents – there is little doubt about the devastating consequences when the family is disrupted.

For the modern family of the '90s, it seems to be the best of times and the worst of times. Never before have so many done so much for the family and children. Yet, at the same time, today's family is assaulted by divorce, violence, poverty, and an increasingly complex and hostile world that seems poised to defeat its very structure.

The family is the fundamental root of society, the foundation that defines our culture and our community. In her book, *Dr. Mom's Parenting Guide,* Dr. Marianne Neifert says:

> The family is the first setting in which socialization takes place and where children learn to live with mutual respect for one another. A family is where a child learns to display affection, control his temper, and pick up his toys. Finally, a family is a perpetual source of encouragement, advocacy, assurance, and emotional refueling that empowers a child to venture with confidence into the greater world and to become all that he can be.[3]

But this ideal isn't being realized. In fact, because so many of today's families are disrupted, the nuclear family is breaking down. Therefore, we can expect lack of respect, lack of affection, discouragement, problems with temper and behavior, lack of confidence, and so on. Children never do realize their full potential.

Because of this chronic deterioration in family relationships, kids are in a double bind. They are caught in the struggle of realizing they need to be closer and attached to their parents, but it's easier to push the adults away.

And unwittingly, the adults are playing into this struggle. Technology is enabling the family to polarize. There used to be "simple" outside-the-home activities – second jobs, school functions, athletic practices, dance classes – that kept the family from spending quality time together. But today it is not uncommon to have each family member relegated to a corner of the house being "entertained" by TV, computer games, Walkmans,® Internet surfing, Game Boys,® etc. Few families "surf the net" on the same board.

In fact, it's rare for family members to have quality interactions even in the confinement of the family car, with the radio blasting in the front seat, kids with separate headphones and hand-held Game Boys® in the back, Mom or Dad on the cell phone bringing the office "on the road."

These "distancing phenomena" become ironic. Most modern parents who want their kids to be socially acceptable and current with popular trends probably don't realize that, in fact, what they have provided for their children are new, advanced vehicles that *empower the children to control the distance in the parent-child relationship.*

And moreover, this distancing is occurring when the adults and kids are feeling *good* about each other. This tendency and opportunity to distance is exaggerated when difficult feelings and situations need to be worked out between parents and children. Technology has given the children more opportunity and social permission to isolate themselves emotionally whenever they choose.

The choice to distance may be purposeful or not. Either way, the child is defended and may be afraid the relationship won't work. In other words, she is saying, "I know you will let me down in the end, so let's get it over with." Then she acts out this dynamic.

For every success story such as Donald's, I have worked with teens who have never "made it." Some become homeless, unable to keep jobs or relationships; others get into bad relationships, have kids, and repeat the cycle.

They have never allowed themselves to love or be loved. Because of either their own defended strategy or adult reactions to them, they failed or were denied the opportunity to "practice" successful relationships with their parents. They couldn't break the cycle of not being able to *feel* loved and accepted – they couldn't "let it in," and adults didn't know how to "get it in."

I have seen first-hand what we all see on the evening news: the lives of kids and families being forever scarred by broken, even violent marriages; crime and death because of drug use; and individual and gang violence on the streets and in our schools. The disturbing questions of "why" and "what happened" haunt all of us who care about our kids.

Chapter 2

"Because I said so, that's why!"

Most people parent the way *they* were parented. This is understandable, given that modeling is the most powerful teacher. I have seen so many sincere parents who have consciously and knowingly vowed to "not do to my child what was done to me!" Yet, when they are in the heat of battle, experiencing the intense emotions associated with dealing with their children, they invariably revert to doing "what worked with me for my parents."

True, this is sometimes a very sound and effective socialization process as family values, attitudes and beliefs are passed on to each generation. But more often, the context within which that imprinting took place has radically changed.

The truth is: My children are not me, and I am not my parents. We are each different individuals within a very different reality. I believe these differences need to be understood by parents, and that each child's uniqueness needs to be considered when they are being parented. And, to emphasize the point, many parenting styles we see "out there" being modeled and passed on generation to generation should be retired.

One such parenting style is what I call the "Charge of the Light Brigade" approach. With this approach, the parent believes she has a complete understanding – right or wrong – of what is best for the child. "Yours is not to reason why…"

Unfortunately, while this method can be expedient, it can deprive the child of the ability to make decisions and individuate – the necessary process for becoming an individual. This can leave the child with serious questions about self-worth and the ability to function independently in society.

At some point, he starts to question the parental values that don't seem to fit for him and react accordingly. He will either become compliant or rebellious – both reactions being two sides of the same wrong coin. Both are adaptations to parental coercion and *not* the beginnings of the child's own internalized set of values.

This reaction can happen at every developmental stage. It would manifest for a 2-year-old as the parent insisting that the child play with *this* puzzle instead of *those* blocks. For a 16-year-old, it's the parents insisting that the teen must have *these* friends instead of *those,* must look *this* way instead of *that.*

So, should the child have free reign, be able choose whatever? Of course not. (Later, we'll discuss the Partnership Model of Discipline.) My point, simply stated, is that when the "I'm-the-boss-and-you're-not" approach is used, it is ultimately ineffective.

Whenever the adult gives the message – literally or covertly – that the child must behave as the adult mandates – without *child's* needs being considered – then alienation has begun. "I know what is best for you, you will do it, and you will like it." (This message is really for the convenience or satisfaction of the adult.)

The child can hear this message at different levels, from the seemingly minor day-to-day interactions, to major life-changing decisions. It occurs when the child is:

- sent to his room when he is bad. Rather than working out the problem, the adult doesn't have the time, patience, or energy to struggle and process with him.

- physically, sexually, or emotionally abused as a result of the adults "working out" their internal emotional disturbances.
- given up for adoption when the adult – again – can't or won't struggle with the "burden" of the child.
- severely neglected or abandoned.
- put into foster care (because it's more convenient than…)

We can understand the alienation of our children (and why there is a love disorder) on the societal level: it is caused by the breakdown of the nuclear family and the implementation of distancing phenomena to help insulate the child from having to relate. But more specific to the alienation, we must consider the adult-child relationship. Is the "boss" really making the right decision in the interest of the child – or merely charging into battle – or worse, avoiding the battle altogether?

Chapter 3

The Shrinking Safety Zone

Through all the conflict, chaos and isolation, it is remarkable that most teens end up on a spot somewhere in the middle of the continuum marked "normal." Although most arrive safely, they carry some scars – badges of transition to learn from or repeat as adults. Those teens who act out the societal and family breakdown, along with their own sense of alienation, find themselves on the extremes, out of balance, and termed "high risk" and "abnormal."

On the other extreme of "at-risk" behavior is the teen who "acts-in." That is, she holds her anxiety in, retreats to her room and stays in her own world, oblivious to healthy interactions. See Figure 1:

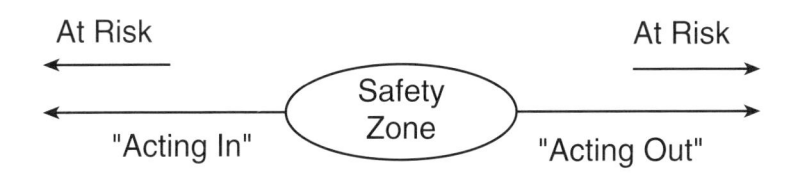

```
   At Risk                                   At Risk
  ←——————                                  ——————→
  ←——————————( Safety Zone )——————————→
   "Acting In"                             "Acting Out"
```

Figure 1

Unfortunately, in today's world, the normal and safe range is shrinking year by year. The dangerous extremes are encroaching, a result of the disintegrating structures of family and community and the assault of technology and complexity. You can read about it daily, hear it on the 5 o'clock news: guns, violence, drugs, teen pregnancy, runaways.

The barrage of screaming headlines is overwhelming: "Killing sprees tied by string of youth rage;"[1] "76 percent of high school students and 46 percent of middle school students say drugs are kept, used, or sold on their school grounds;"[2] "There is an increase in the use of LSD, cocaine and crack;"[3] "More than 1 million young girls a year are becoming teenage mothers;"[4] "Since 1970, the youth suicide-rate has tripled."[5]

The statistics have been repeated to the degree that they are numbing. The volume of information has become so staggering that we lose sight of the individual behind each statistic. Because of the frustration and the powerlessness they feel, it is easy for parents to fall into the traps of clichés: "The whole world is falling apart," followed by the other myths: "In the good old days..." or "Teenagers have always *been* a problem, have always *had* problems;" "I did my best, there's nothing we can do;" or, "It's just a violent world."

In the article "Violent Youth" by Michael Manciaux, he states,

> It is far from certain that violence is more widespread and more frequent in our modern societies than it was in the past. There are no figures enabling us to judge, and even if we had them, any real comparison would be difficult, since the definition of violence itself is highly subjective.[6]

He continues by saying,

> What is sure is that aggression and violence intrude more and more into our daily lives; the instantaneous and worldwide coverage by the media makes sure of that. [7]

Manciaux makes a good point about our exposure to violence *and* our children's exposure, both in fantasy (television, movies) and reality (evening news). But I disagree with his conclusion about violence. The definition of violence may be subjective, but I think we would all agree that the recent increase in drive-by shootings, the escalation of violence, and hate crimes that so many of our nation's metropolitan areas are experiencing are harbingers of things to come.

From my perspective, all teens are "high risk" to some degree. For teenagers, the Safety Zone shrinks too quickly. They become targets in all aspects of their lives, from relationships, to driving, to what they put into their bodies. Parents who were teenagers in the '60s had room to experiment; today, kids' first experiments with sex or drugs could be their last. Even those who stay clear of gangs and guns are sometimes winding up as innocent victims caught in the crossfire. If you haven't been to a high school recently (or even a junior high), here's a quick snapshot of the obstacle course teens maneuver through daily. The Big Three: sex, drugs, and – no, not rock'n'roll – violence.

Bang! Bang! You're Next

Schools have always battled the infiltration of violence and gangs. Today, because of the availability of handguns and the glamorization of gangs, violence has reached epidemic proportions. I don't want to get bogged down in the statistics, but I do want to paint the alarming picture that is developing.

The National League of Cities reported that school violence in the year 1995 resulted in student deaths or injuries in 41 percent of American cities with populations of 100,000 or more.[8]

Since 1996, there has been an alarming increase in the number of violent, deadly shootings by teens. In February 1996, a high school student killed three people in his algebra class. In October 1997, another student killed three and wounded seven at his high school. And recently, yet another student 15, killed four and wounded 22 in a shooting rampage that started at his home and ended at his high school.

A number of patterns have emerged from these killings:
- In each case, the child felt picked on or inferior.
- Each had above-average intelligence.
- The killers had easy access to high-powered guns.
- According to reports, the killers seemed to be obsessed by violent pop culture in some way.
- The killers each gave warning signals.[9]

To this list, I would add that there is a high probability that each of the killers suffered from attachment issues.

- 16.6 percent of students polled said they had carried a gun to school within the past 30 days.
- Every 92 seconds, an American child is shot.
- Every school day, more than 150,000 students stay home because they are sick of violence and afraid of being stabbed, shot, or beaten.
- 57 percent of public elementary and secondary school principals reported that one or more

incidents of crime/violence occurred in their schools during the 1996/1997 school year.
- In 1995, 2.7 million violent crimes took place at or near schools.
- In 1997, 13,076 students in the U.S. were suspended daily from school for violence.
- Some 6,093 students were expelled during the 1996/1997 school year for bringing firearms to school.[10]

Behind each statistic is a story. In January 1997, 14-year-old John Kamel died at the hands of another 14-year-old, Tronneal Mangum. Why did Mangum do it? Kamel thought Mangum stole his watch, and he wanted it back. A young witness told police, "Kamel wanted his watch back. He said, 'Hey, give me my watch.' Then boom, boom, boom."

Then Mangum walked away. Witnesses did not say that he ran away in a panic at what he had done. He simply walked away.

Leonard Pitts, a columnist for *The Miami Herald*, comments on this case in an editorial titled, "School tragedy's bitter lesson: Society's coldness has created kids who don't feel." In his column, Pitts writes:

> Death seems such a casual thing these days, violence capricious and easy, mindless rage never far from the surface. We teach children that in our homes, show it to them in our streets, entertain them with it on television. And then are surprised when some of them become killers. Or killed.[11]

The June 1997 issue of *People* magazine asks the question in its cover story: "Why are kids killing?" According to the article, the number of murders committed by teenagers during the past decade has "leaped from 1,000 a year to nearly 4,000."[12]

What is terribly disturbing is that more and more young people involved in these violent acts are lacking the capacity to make connections with another life. As Dr. David Hartman, the director of neuropsychology at the Isaac Ray Center for Psychiatry and Law in Chicago, states, "They need have no more reason for hurting another human being than they have for peeling an orange."[13] Here is another description that could be applied to Donald and his need to protect his "stuff."

So, how much is society to blame for this "coldness"? Who is responsible for these kids who "don't feel," and what can be done about them? In the next chapter, we'll explore causal factors and then discuss possible interventions.

Turn On, Tune In, Drop Dead

The Baby-Boomer Counterculture recently lost two of its own: Jerry Garcia and Timothy Leary. In their halcyon days, Leary was inviting a generation to "turn on," and Jerry, guitar in hand, did. And, of course, both paid for their "wild, crazy ride." As icons, they represented a curious paradox: they were both admired and scorned. Those parents who followed them through that "long, strange trip" of the '60s now find themselves in the dubious position of lecturing their own teenagers about the perils of drugs. And, also, of course, many of these teens are pointing at Jerry and Timothy and scoffing, "Yeah, right, Dad. Just say 'no' the way you did, huh?"

Apparently, not enough teens are saying "no" today. According to the Office of National Drug Policy, Pulse Check Treatment providers report that approximately one-third of all clients in treatment for marijuana abuse are under 20. They also report an increase in the number of young clients who abuse inhalants."[14]

As one 15-year-old girl stated, "If you don't do drugs, you don't have any fun." In the survey, teenagers said drugs are "hip" and "readily available." On a positive note, however, teen use is down from the all-time high: in 1979, 14.2 percent of youths had used marijuana.[15]

One other disturbing trend was identified: Pre-teen drug use is on the upswing. California's Ventura County Deputy District Attorney Bell Redmond has spoken of the problem that is pervasive in every community in America, whether urban or rural. The most significant trend regarding drugs is that no community is immune.[16]

Sex Is Not a Four-Letter Word

Regarding sex and teenagers, there is good news, and there is not-so-good news. The good news is that, according to the U.S. Department of Health and Human Services, teenage birth rates (teenagers having babies) have declined over the past few years.[17]

The unfortunate news? Part of this decline may be the result of increased abortion rates. Four of every 10 American women are pregnant by age 20, the highest ratio of any industrialized country. Statistics on pregnancy report that there are 1,300 teenage births and 1,000 teenage abortions each day. In 1997, teenage births absorbed more than $7 billion of public spending.[18]

Why are kids having kids? Why are they forfeiting their teen years of socializing, dating, and new freedom for changing diapers, early morning feedings, and the ultimate responsibility?

Interestingly enough, a new poll shows that Americans overwhelmingly favor teen celibacy.[19] And in another survey, more than 90 percent of teenage girls said understanding parents, self-respect, careful choice of boyfriends, and being informed about and using birth control could help prevent pregnancies.[20]

Still, the teen birth rate is reaching epidemic proportions. And, research shows that "families headed by single women with children are the poorest of all demographic groups regardless of how poverty is measured.[21] *Epidemic.* The word sounds ominous, like a disease. What *should* be a joyous occasion – having a baby – too often becomes a burden, a family disruption, then, finally, a statistic. The difference between "having children" and "being a parent" is as disparate as the difference between throwing a bullet and shooting one.

My introduction to teen pregnancy caught me completely off-guard. I was in my second year of teaching, still fresh, idealistic; my students seemed to be having a good time. I felt like I was making a difference.

One of the games I used to play with my class was the "Map Game," a quick exercise where I'd call out a location on the map, call on a student, hand them the pointer and watch them struggle to find Belize or Tierra del Fuego. When the class was sagging, it always energized the room.

One morning, we were playing, and the kids were hopping up and down, passing the pointer, laughing. I called on Sherry, a shy 15-year-old who'd always had a tough time with school.

"Argentina," I called out, holding out the pointer. She didn't move. "Sherry," I prompted. She hugged herself and shook her head. I knew she knew where it was, and usually she enjoyed the game.

"Pass?" I offered. She nodded. I called on someone else and made a note to talk with her after class. As she was leaving, I called her to my desk.

"Sherry, are you okay?"

She nodded, looked down at her shoes, pulled her books to her chest as her eyes teared up.

"What's going on?"

She shook her head. "I can't tell you."

"Are you sick?"

She shook her head again, wildly.

"Was the map question too hard?" I stood up and pointed to South America. "I know you know where Argentina – "

"I'm pregnant," she blurted.

"Oh," I said, stepping back from the map. No wonder she didn't care about Argentina. A flurry of questions ran through my mind. Who? What? How pregnant…why? My education classes never really prepared me for something like this. I wasn't sure what to do.

"Who's the father?" She continued to sob. I stepped around the desk and guided her to a seat. I thought about the boy I'd seen her with in the halls. "Is it Timmy?"

She nodded. "Oh." Great, I thought. Fifteen-year-old Timmy who had never turned in a homework assignment in his life, who couldn't find his own seat with two hands. Timmy was going to be a father.

"Does your mother know?"

She shook her head "no" again.

"It's okay," I said in a quiet voice. "Here's what we're going to do." I set up a time to meet with Sherry and her mom, and during the next months, I got an education on teen pregnancy.

I was shocked when I met Sherry's mom; she was an older version of Sherry: quiet, with short brown hair, timid smile, and barely 31. And now she was going to be a grandmother.

The story was fairly simple and self-revealing. Sherry's mom had gotten pregnant when she was 15, had never married, and now Sherry was repeating the cycle. She intended to keep the baby, drop out of school, and have her mom help her raise her new son or daughter.

"What about the dad…Timmy? Is he – "

"He's not welcome in the house," Sherry's mom said, suddenly indignant.

That was more than 15 years ago. I lost touch with Sherry after she had the baby (a girl). She promised me she'd get her Graduate Equivalency Degree. I don't think she did. I can only wonder if she's a grandmother now, her mom a great-grandmother at 46. Fortunately, Sherry had a support system. At least her baby had a home and a family.

For many, there is no support system. Ready or not, the baby comes, the teen mother is ill-prepared, and the baby becomes a "burden" that keeps the family mired in poverty.

Chapter 4

Aliens on a Small Planet

The problem? More kids today are engaging more often in more intense "high-risk" behaviors. I think there are more adolescents at risk of becoming lost or dangerous to society today than ever before. I believe part of the reason is that they feel more alienated from adults, school, and peers, and there is more deep despair.

As Alvin Toffler states in his book, *Future Shock*,[1] for people today – especially the adolescent – the future is coming faster than they can handle it. Society is becoming more reliant on technology and less so on interpersonal relations. There is too much distance between children – teens, in particular – and their parents, teachers, and other significant adults.

Since every parent and child are trying to connect, some of the distance/alienation is the normal, natural separation needed to individuate. Yet, *some of this distance is a learned response to the pain of not getting needs met.* Moreover, there are certainly many external factors – such as the decline of the nuclear family – that increases separation.

There is a pseudo-sophistication among adolescents. Teens are exposed to more and more, equipped with less and less, and at an increasingly younger age. Sex education is one example. According to the Guttmacher Institute, "American adolescents are no more sexually active than their counterparts in Sweden, Holland, France, Canada and Britain but are many times more likely to become pregnant."[2]

Why? One reason, states *Rocky Mountain News* editorial writer Linda Seabach, is obvious: "One of the few things that everyone agrees on is that teenage sex is more common than it used to be."[3] The Sexuality Information and Education Council of the United States says that in the 1950s, about 25 percent of women 18 or older had intercourse; today that number is estimated to be 56 percent. Seventy-five percent of men over 18 are estimated to be sexually active.[4]

Ironically, while we may not talk openly to kids about sex at school or at home, we have no trouble displaying it. The average teen can come home, jump on the Internet, and have acces to more than 1,700,00 matches for sex topics. So, is sex education the answer? How about passing out condoms at school? While the debate rages between the Religious Right and the Liberal Left, teens continue to get pregnant, babies continue to be born…ready or not.

These facts are, in large part, the result of teens feeling unheard, uncounted, and unloved. My point is that we haven't done a very good job of communicating, of understanding teens and their needs. Why aren't we dicussing morals and teaching about contraceptives? We should be helping our teenagers understand the alternatives to and the consequences of sexual activity. Certainly, if we had better communication and trust, we could. I also think part of the problem *is* that pseudo-sophistication mentioned earlier: teens look like adults, they have jobs like adults, they have sex like adults…but we know that, emotionally, they are still kids.

The kids we are describing here – those acting out in various degrees of at-risk behavior with sex, drugs, and violence – feel alienated. Their quality of attachment was disrupted for whatever variety of reasons. They are searching for identity and the safety to pursue and develop it. They will seek out someone or some vehicle (gangs, cults) to attach to and find themselves, so we'd better provide the best parent/role models possible.

Donald's attachment was continuously disrupted during his first five years. He was abused, neglected, and, finally, abandoned by his mother. After being adopted, he settled in with his new family, letting them get close – but not too close. His defense system kept him safe; however, he was also seen professionally at this point and received diagnoses that labeled him "oppositional defiant," "hostile," and "passive aggressive."

Donald was stuck in a cycle in which he was incapable of attaching to positive role models: his adoptive parents, teachers, the "system." Instead, it was much easier to attach to a crowd that believed much as he did: get high, numb the pain, no responsibility, no expectations. This was all as a response to his birth mother, who had parented "conveniently." Donald's acting out was a response to her approach of, "Because I said so, that's why!"

Donald was an alien in a world he didn't understand, that didn't understand him. The rules didn't make sense because, ultimately, he didn't – *couldn't* – trust anyone. Once he let me in, we found the tear in his attachment… *and* a way to mend it.

The only thing harder today than being the *parent* of a teenager is *being* a teenager. I've raised four children, and they all passed through the Twilight Zone of adolescence – if not unscathed, at least intact. The teen years are wild, exciting, confusing, and lonely – sometimes all at once. These kids are caught in a vortex of change: their bodies, the rules, their relationships, how they fit in, *if* they'll fit in.

On the one hand, they feel pulled toward the end of the spectrum that represents conformity, rules, structure, discipline, their parents' values. Tugging on the opposite end of the spectrum is the invitation to rebellion. One of the toughest concepts I see teens – and parents of teens – struggling with is the paradox between following the rules and rebelling. Teens need to rebel; it's part of individuation – how they grow and develop and become their own person.

That said, and as a parent who survived the Teen Wars, I often found myself mumbling, "Isn't there a way they can rebel quietly? Within the rules? Maybe with a good haircut, or at least a job?" The answer, of course, is more often "no" than "yes." Change is difficult, sometimes violent. The process of self-discovery is a perilous balancing act between acceptance and rebellion, self-expression and conformity.

Donald was caught between these tensions. Because of the disruptions in his life, he developed defensive strategies to protect himself. As he got older, he became the epitome of a parent's worst nightmare, the poster child of the "Horrible Teenager."

I first met Donald when he was 14 and going nowhere. He slunk into my office, leaned his skinny body against the door jamb and stared out past his long, stringy brown hair. He looked like a typical "skater." When I said "hello" he didn't respond, and he avoided eye contact. It was clear: I was the enemy.

Donald's file read like hundreds of other teenagers in trouble: oppositional defiant, history of pot; he'd tried LSD. He had also been diagnosed with Attention Deficit Disorder and was on Ritalin®. He'd been adopted at 5, and his history in school from that time forward was marked with discipline problems. When we met, he had just been released from a hospital where he'd been sent after getting caught smoking pot. As soon as he was released, he got caught smoking again. (So much for the rehab program.)

Donald was obviously bright. He had good social skills but used them to con people. His motto was, "I don't care." After talking to him for five minutes, I realized his attitude was, "And what are YOU gonna' do about it?"

The first 10 minutes of our session was fairly typical. Donald had an answer for everything – or a way to use his silence as an answer. Then something remarkable happened. Whether it was because I seemed harmless, or because it was just the right time in his life, he opened up just a bit. We were discussing his drug use, and I offered that I understood that he was medicating his pain.

"Whaddaya mean?' he returned, angrily.

"I know you're hurting, and you're trying to find a way to make it stop. But getting high won't work."

He frowned for a moment, then suddenly looked away.

"Do you want some help?" I asked, softly.

He nodded and started crying.

At that moment, Donald showed me his core. What I saw in that glimpse was his genuineness, depth, his desire to be understood. Without a doubt, there was something about him worth reaching: he had admitted he was hurting and that he wanted help, and my challenge was to find a way in.

During the next two years, we struggled through an arduous process in which we developed a working relationship. I believed that the best way to reach Donald's core was to examine his early attachments and family "ties." He seemed to be suffering from the disruption of the attachments that he so desperately needed.

How did these disruptions occur? What were the effects on Donald? Were these disruptions the reason he needed to protect his core? And finally, even though he had shown me his core on that first day, could it actually be reached so he would let me in? The answers to these and other questions will be found in the understanding of the next chapter, which more fully describes Attachment Theory: the "ties that should bind."

Section Two
Love Is A Many Splendored Thing...If

...if it can be experienced for what it is, and if it can flow in, out, and between people. In order to live in the splendor of love through each developmental milestone of growing up, children need an environment that fulfills the original, innate blueprint of how love is supposed to work. When that "little bundle of id" (the infant) cries to get her needs met — and that natural, "built-in" request mechanism is met with a loving, caring response from the caregiver — a relationship begins. When this cycle is repeated consistently over the first two years of life, an attachment is formed. Over time, the attachment becomes an enduring emotional tie between the infant and caregiver, which the child begins to rely upon to feel safe and secure.

The quality of the attachment may actually be observed in the child. Indications of attachment may be seen as she experiences the distress of separation from the caregiver, the joy of being reunited with her, and when the child seeks closeness with the caregiver when needing to be protected. The patterns of interaction that are established early on for the child will be the "style" she will use in subsequent loving relationships. So whatever the child experiences with the caregiver in those crucial first two years, it will be repeated "moreso" as she expands her relationships. If her blueprint for loving relationships is fulfilled with a secure attachment, the actual basis for her love being "many splendored" is set.

Chapter 5

The Ties That Should Bind

Perhaps the most significant bond that we humans experience is the least understood: the infant-mother bond. During the past quarter-century, modern psychology has opened an entire new chapter on the bonding process. From John Bowlby's definitive attachment trilogy, *Attachment and Loss,* to Dr. Foster Cline's *Hope for High Risk and Rage Filled Children,* to Robert Karen's *Becoming Attached,* the body of research and theory continues to expand. Yet, psychologists and theorists are still at odds about interpretation and, more importantly, about how to use the information practically.

First, in order to understand "attachment," we must address the distinction between instinct, bonding, and attachment.

Typically, "instinct" is the term applied to animal behaviors by ethologists. As Robert Karen points out in *Becoming Attached,* "Darwin...devotes a chapter of *The Origin of Species* to animal behaviors, noting that each species has its own peculiar repertoire of instinctual behavior patterns, which are as fundamental to the species as its anatomy."[1]

He clarifies this definition by pointing out that a species-specific behavior is instinctive, but it is not preordained. "The song a chaffinch will sing is limited to a creation range and quality by its genetic predisposition. But it must hear the song of an adult chaffinch if its song is to develop at all."[2] (This idea is a good response to the nature/nurture debate; it is not an either/or proposition.)

Perhaps the most recognizable example of this behavior is imprinting. This has been demonstrated with newly hatched ducks waddling after their surrogate psychologist- "mother," Konrad Lorenz, complete with lab coat and unwebbed feet. Ducks bond with the first moving object they see; likewise, if ducks do not see moving objects within approximately 12 hours after hatching, normal bonding will not take place.[3]

John Bowlby, considered one of the pioneers of attachment theory, recognized the correlation between animal and human behavior. He reasoned that people, too, had bonding behaviors and intergenerational cues – and that the environment played a crucial role in determining the outcome. He concluded that "..sucking, clinging, following, crying and smiling are all part of the child's instinctual repertoire, whose goal is to keep the mother close by."[4]

Bowlby also made the distinction between bonding and attachment. He introduced the word "attachment" to describe the infant-mother bond. While bonding suggested an instantaneous event, "attachment suggested a complex, developing process."[5] He saw attachment as much more akin to the process of learning to give and receive love, leading to an enduring emotional tie between the infant and caregiver.[6]

Also, during the baby's first year, he wrote, "the child is gradually able to display a complete range of 'attachment behaviors,' protesting mother's departure, greeting her returns, clinging when frightened, following when able."[7]

These "behaviors" were also supported by Harry Harlow's experiments with Rhesus monkeys. He found that when the infant monkey was frightened, it sought a terry cloth artificial mother that provided no food as opposed to a wire-framed artificial mother that provided milk. This suggests that attachment can transcend – and is superior to – survival instincts.[8]

In his first volume, *Attachment and Loss,* Bowlby introduced a revolutionary view of the infant-caregiver bond. He asserted: "Attachment is not a motive derived from mother's association with food, nor is it part of the human sexuality. Rather, the disposition to become attached is an independent system, built into primate biology to ensure survival."[9]

Attachment theory, as developed by Bowlby, formulates a way to think of and explain the need for human beings to make strong affectional bonds to particular others. It also includes the many forms of emotional distress and disturbances – which include anxiety, anger and depression – to which unwilling separation and loss gives rise.[10]

The key words here are "particular others." While the importance of the mother/child bond has long been recognized as the *key* affectional bond, the role of the family – even the definition of family, particularly as we head into the 21st Century – continues to shift as it is redefined. Other aspects of the theory that have not yet been agreed upon are the specific effects the early relationship has on further personality development and behavior in the older child and in the adult.

Attachment theory integrates psychoanalytic, social learning, and ethological theories (the study of behavior from a biological point of view) to explain how the bond between infant and mother develops and serves as the foundation for *all* future encounters and relationships. However, attachment theory does *not* accept the premise of psychoanalytic and social learning theory that the affectional drive is a secondary one, derived from the gratification of primary physiological needs. In other words, the infant doesn't just develop good feelings for the mother or the caregiver because she feeds and nurtures the baby. The attachment between the infant and the caregiver is formed as an independent system, complete with its own set of complex responses that exist independently of the more simple feeding-gratitude response.

Still, I believe an examination of recent research and studies by Bowlby, Ainsworth, Rutter, Bell and Harlow provides convincing evidence that the strong attachment process between infant and mother/caregiver is crucial for normal development.

Chapter 6

Those Crucial First Two Years

In her book, *Every Child's Birthright: In Defense of Maternity,* Thelma Fraiberg tells us that "children who have been deprived of mothering and who have formed no personal human bonds during the first two years of life, show permanent impairment of the capacity to make human attachments in later childhood, even when substitute families are provided for them. The degree of impairment is roughly equivalent to the degree of deprivation."[1]

Fraiberg goes on to tell us that human infancy is the critical period for the establishment of human bonds. John Bowlby dates the approximate beginnings of attachment to the second half of the first year of life. The strength of the attachment between infant and mother reaches its peak during the second year, and the attachment is normally achieved by the end of the third year.[2]

Secondary attachments to new figures become possible as the maturing child turns from the embrace of his mother to his expanding social world. Here, the role of the "particular others" is especially crucial in defining how that child's social world develops. He forms attachments to people who are available – emotionally and physically – to bring comfort during times of stress, regardless of who meets his actual needs. The quality of *sensitive responsiveness* being consistently offered by those who are available to help him during these uncomfortable times seems to be the single most important factor in his being able to form secure attachments.[3]

Dr. Foster Cline is another notable pioneer in both the theory and treatment of children with attachment disruptions. Regarding infant bonding, he states that the ingredients for bonding – which is the foundation for all interaction – include a subtle combination of three factors:

1. Genetic and intrauterine factors
2. Early maternal-infant interaction patterns that form basic trust
3. Parenting and/or therapy during toddlerhood that forms the sense of autonomy[4]

All three are crucial in the development of a healthy, well-adjusted child. Likewise, breaks can occur in any of the three, which then result in attachment issues.[5]

Genetics play a role as well as the environment. The controversy of nature vs. nurture as the determining factor of influence is a useless one because both are critical; again, it is not a "one or the other" argument.

The essence of Cline's theory is illustrated in what he terms "The Soul Cycle" – or what attachment therapists typically call "the Attachment Cycle." According to Cline, this cycle rolls around every four hours as the infant is fed. By the time the baby is 6 months old, it has been completed hundreds of times. Cline writes, "The cycle 'locks in' our first associational patterns. These patterns stick with us all of our lives. Although unconscious, these associations dictate many of our actions."[6]

We also know that an infant learns half a lifetime's knowledge in the first year of life.[7] She also learns to be secure or insecure, to laugh or mainly cry and whine – which, in turn, determines the subsequent response from the caregivers. The status of the Attachment Cycle then determines not only the blueprint for the child, but the quality of her relationships, starting with the first caregivers.

I would add that, given all the other physiological needs – i.e., touch, warmth, breath, bodily elimination, plus the myriad psychological needs – rootedness, safety, belonging, nurturing, etc. – the infant is in a *constant* state of need. In other words, rather than repeating every four hours, the Attachment Cycle is constant. See Figure 2:

The Attachment Cycle

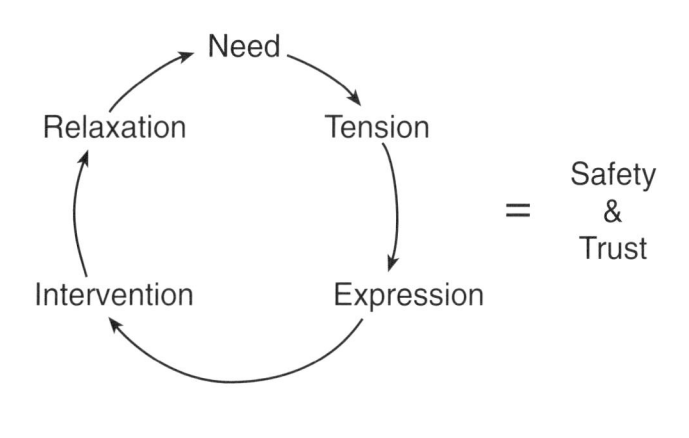

Need → Tension → Expression → Intervention → Relaxation → Need

= Safety & Trust

Figure 2

As the child becomes needy, he no longer feels safe. He enters a state of tension/arousal (fight or flight/kill or be killed). "Am I going to die if I don't get my needs met? If I don't get fed?"

The tension gives rise to an expression of the discomfort the child is experiencing. For an infant, that expression is typically rage.

Ideally, the expression is met with a parental intervention intended to satisfy the need. If the intervention is successful, the child relaxes and feels safe and secure. He feels that he can survive and can trust that his caregivers will help him get his needs met.

At the most basic level, the infant has two jobs: crying and cooing, i.e., smiling, making "goo-goo" noises, being generally cute. When babies are "in-tune" with Mom, they will cry with such clarity that she (sometimes Dad) can distinguish whether the cry is one of hunger, pain, or a need to be cuddled.

The "coo" is the infant's way of telling Mom "thank you," and "I feel better." This reinforces her feeling of attachment and the mother's motivation to meet her needs. This is the beginning of a healthy, reciprocal relationship.

I agree with Cline when he states, "Presently in America, more children are destroyed by poor infant care and early abuse and neglect than poor genetics."[8] I also agree with his conclusion that, while it is senseless to argue nature vs. nurture, it is "a grievous mistake not to recognize the importance of any of the factors upon which personality rests."[9] The complex variables that combine – or don't combine – during the first two years of life determine the blueprint for that child.

Chapter 7

The "Moreso" Theory
(Filling In The Blueprint)

There is an old concept in developmental psychology called the "Moreso Theory." Simply stated, it asserts that, whatever you *are* now, you will be *moreso* later. Auguste Aichorn, a young man who worked with Sigmund Freud at the Vienna clinic, stated, "Adolescence recapitulates the problems of a 2-year-old."[1]

At our center, Human Passages, we've had many discussions about teenagers – how adolescents are like 2-year-olds with hormones and wheels. It's an accurate comparison, since both 2-year-olds and adolescents are working on individuation and autonomy. The cycle the child internalizes at age 2 will be "moreso" at age 14.

To illustrate, I'd like to share the story of a couple – we'll call them Jim and Marsha – and their journey as parents from the birth of their son to his teenage years. Jim and Marsha were a young couple in their late 20s; both had good jobs, and they had a stable relationship. A year before they decided to "get pregnant," they both went on a fast to purify their bodies. Marsha maintained a healthy diet through pregnancy, complete with pre-natal vitamins. Once they found out they were pregnant, they attended birthing classes, perused the latest research, subscribed to *Parent Magazine,* and read everything from Dr. Benjamin Spock to Dr. Berry Brazelton.

During the pregnancy, they both continued to exercise. They compiled family advice and folk remedies, started buying bonds for a college fund, had the bedroom colors picked for both a boy or a girl. (They asked the doctor, after the ultra-sound, not to reveal the baby's sex.)

After a difficult pregnancy with complications, Marsha had a C-section and delivered an 8 pound, 7 ounce boy whom they named Tyler. Tyler had a rough first few months of life: he was sick, colicky, and had ear infections. At 4 months, he went into the hospital for three days.

I was invited to Tyler's first birthday party. After the candles were blown out and the cake was cut, I had a chance to talk to Jim. He said he loved being a dad, but it was much more difficult than he had expected. He was a little worried about Tyler. "He's got such a temper. Sometimes he's hard to control. Marsha gets real frustrated and sometimes gets depressed."

About six months later, I got a call from Jim. "Tyler's having temper tantrums. We don't know what to do. He had a fit in the store because he wanted this toy, so I finally gave it to him so he'd quit screaming." Jim sounded tired and frustrated. They couldn't get Tyler to sleep in his own bed; he was throwing fits; Marsha felt she couldn't control him; and since she had started back to work full-time, she felt guilty about not spending enough time with Tyler. Jim wanted to start time-out; Marsha wasn't comfortable with it. "Is this what being a dad is?" Jim asked, laughing nervously.

I assured him that much of what he was experiencing was normal, and then we talked about some techniques to help with Tyler. Our main discussion centered around the Moreso Theory. "What's that?" Jim asked. "I've read all the books and never heard of that."

"You probably haven't," I said, as I explained.

"That's it?" he asked, somewhat underwhelmed with the theory.

"That's enough for now," I said. "Fight your battles now, or you'll never make it through the teen years." We then discussed some simple strategies and techniques (listed later in this book).

    The results were predictable. I didn't hear from Jim or Marsha for about 10 years. Then one day, I got a call from Jim. Tyler had been kicked out of school; he was hanging with a rough crowd of teenagers. He ignored Marsha, and Jim felt like Tyler hated him. What had happened?

    I didn't remind Jim about our "Moreso" discussion.

Chapter 8

A "Security" Deposit

We know that the first two years of a child's life are the most crucial in determining either a secure attachment or an insecure one. By age 3, he enters into a period of "goal-corrected partnership" with his mother.[1] About this time, he begins to substantially understand some things about his mother's plans for achieving her goals for him. The child, then, is able to modify his attachment behavior to respond to the needs and pleasures of his mother.

As the child slowly forms an idea of herself and others, she creates working models of how the world and others in it may be expected to behave and what she may expect of herself. Every day in my practice, I hear exasperated parents complaining about their out-of-control teenagers. "She acted the same way when he was 2. She didn't listen then, she doesn't listen now!" This is the adolescent stage of the Moreso Theory. The battle that wasn't resolved at age 2 has resurfaced.

From birth, the child constantly creates a blueprint for the future formulated from how each caregiver responds. He may view his first attachment figures as sensitively responsive, consistent, and dependable – or as inadequately responsive, inconsistent, and capricious. *Individuals tend to perceive and respond to new relationships in old ways, often despite the quality and security of the new relationship.*

Thus, throughout childhood, the dynamics of the attachment cycle repeat thousands of times. Even into the teen years, they will surface and constantly repeat, but you may have to look hard to see them working.

For example (using the terminology from the Attachment Cycle diagram on p. 31): A teen is having difficulty completing homework (need) and has slipped into a negative cycle of avoidance and lying behavior to cover up. He is afraid to talk to his teacher to try and solve the issue in order to ease the discomfort of the tension. The parent senses the problem (through teen's expressions) and then attempts to help the student come up with possible strategies for solving the problem (intervention).

Together, the student and the parent develop a plan. For example, they set up a special study area, set a specific time to do homework, do the work he understands first, etc. If the intervention is successful, the tension is reduced (relaxation), he feels safer and more trusting, and is back on track. The quality of the relationship is enhanced (attachment increases) through increased feelings of trust, safety, and nurturing. This tension/expression/intervention/relaxation cycle is constantly being repeated, even *moreso,* just as it did when he was an infant.

What does all this mean? Research tells us that, within this framework of symbolic models, the child – and later adult – makes predictions about the availability and responsiveness of her caregivers. The response of the caregivers serves as a mirror to the child and gives her feedback about the worthiness of her core (love).

A child's being able to feel confident about the availability of the attachment figure provides him with a haven of safety.[2] The attachment figure provides a secure physiological – and later psychological – base from which he can feel safe in unfamiliar environments or situations. The secure child has learned to explore with confidence since he has been assured that his caregivers are readily available. The strength of the attachment is the security deposit on the future. When he experiences this security consistently over time, he is freed to master other life skills beyond survival.

I agree with attachment theorist Michael Rutter as he concludes in his work on attachment and social relationships that competence and autonomy develop as the child's own initiative and exploration leads to favorable-yet-safe results. Besides having a major impact on a child's emotional development, the formation of a healthy, secure attachment is of critical importance in the successful development of other aspects of personality, such as self-esteem, willingness to risk, and sense of humor.[3]

Child developmentalists have investigated and found significant correlations between the quality of attachment and subsequent developmental outcomes. Through the development of an early attachment assessment, it is now possible to successfully predict later levels of functioning in the areas of competence, impulse control, curiosity, problem-solving and socialization.[4] In other words, when the seed is carefully planted, tended, watered, and given a safe, nurturing environment, the flower will grow and eventually bloom.

The research is clear: children with secure attachment are more likely to be enthusiastic, persistent and effective when dealing with life's difficulties than are children with anxious attachment. They are also more resourceful, curious, socially involved, and competent because of the secure foundation their attachments have given them.[5]

This security of attachment allows children who have attained it to learn more quickly and to use adult assistance without becoming overly dependent on it. Children who have had their attachment-processes disrupted are less free to involve themselves in problem-solving.[6] Anxiously attached children are preoccupied with gaining caretaker approval and attention, which becomes a consistent distraction from freely exploring and learning from their environment.

One indication of the quality of a secure attachment is how children react to separation and loss. Bowlby was among those attachment theorists who developed a continuum to depict responses to separation and loss common to children with healthy attachments.[7] Diagnosticians and researchers use the appearance of these responses as indicators of the nature of attachment between child and mother figure. Reactions are identified in three stages: protest, despair, and – finally – detachment.

The first phase, protest, occurs immediately upon separation and is characterized by an intensification of attachment behaviors: a decrease in exploration, arousal of anger, and pushing away. Every new parent experiences this to some degree the first time they drop the baby off at the new day-care center: the baby cries, protests, and is subsequently soothed and held by the "new" caregiver until she is comforted and relaxes, her needs met.

The second phase, despair, is characterized by an increasing hopelessness, inactivity, withdrawal, and crying that tends to be monotonous, muted, and intermittent. Let's say the same baby suddenly needs to be hospitalized. Every time she protests, her needs aren't met; she lies in her crib unattended for longer periods of time, she waits longer to be held, to be fed. She must find ways to cope with and incorporate her new circumstances. With the familiar suddenly unavailable to her, she no longer feels safe and secure. This creates changes in her attachment cycle – possibly damaging ones – that may be accompanied by feelings of despair.

The last phase of the separation response, detachment, is defined by superficial accepting, sociable and cheerful behavior, and a lack of seeking interaction, proximity, and contact with attachment figures. Distance is now developing between the parent and child, and with it comes pain and mistrust.

Again, let's picture this baby, now a bit older, involved in a custody dispute. She is shuffled from Mom to Dad, to the in-laws, to day care, and back again. She senses the anxiety, the disruptions, and cannot count on having her needs met consistently. In order to protect herself, she responds with varying degrees of either anxious or avoidant behaviors. The anxious child will cling to whomever the caregiver of the day happens to be. The avoidant child will detach and manipulate the environment to try and get her needs met. Both are becoming "at risk."

Upon reunion with primary attachment figures, children typically express ambivalence, anxiety, and anger. Non-recognition and detached behavior are characteristic, as are rejecting, hostile actions. These kinds of behavior upon and after reunion are seen as activations of extreme attachment behaviors – which, ironically, are attempts to discourage further separation. They are also responses to anxiety about future separations.[8]

This brings us back to the Shrinking Safety Zone. See Figure 3:

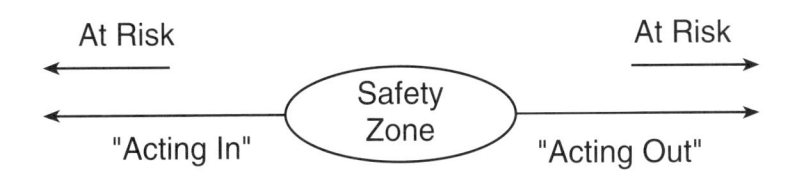

```
     At Risk                                At Risk
   ←――――――                              ――――――→
   ←――――――      ⎛ Safety ⎞             ――――――→
     "Acting In"  ⎝  Zone  ⎠              "Acting Out"
```

Figure 3

In attachment language, the Safety Zone is the area of behavior that is characteristic of children who are securely attached. The increasingly "at risk" behaviors take on the continuum of behaviors that range from children who are anxiously attached to those who are avoidantly attached. See Figure 4:

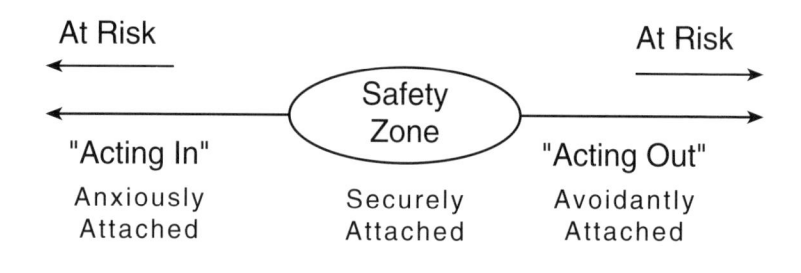

```
     At Risk                                At Risk
  ←————————                              ————————→
  ←————————————(  Safety  )————————————————————→
    "Acting In"  (  Zone   )           "Acting Out"
    Anxiously     Securely              Avoidantly
    Attached      Attached               Attached
```

Figure 4

As the security (safety) decreases and anxiety/avoidance increases, the child becomes more at risk to engage in characteristic behaviors along the continuum. In other words, as the Safety Zone shrinks, parents can count on more extreme behaviors, and, according to the Moreso Theory, things will get worse.

Back to Jim and Marsha: they are good parents; they read all the books, followed all the advice, spent the time and energy to make sure Tyler had all his needs met, and still weren't completely successful. Marsha had a difficult time drawing firm lines with Tyler and wouldn't follow through. Jim repeated the cycle he experienced with his own dad: when things got tough with Tyler, Jim disappeared into his work or was otherwise emotionally unavailable until a crisis erupted.

Whatever Jim's and Marsha's mistakes, they are not atypical first-time parents. The problems with Tyler – tantrums, power struggles about his sleeping in his own bed – were workable issues when he was 2. Since they weren't addressed then, they became more complex and disruptive behaviors at age 14. Instead of smelling Tyler's breath to see if he brushed his teeth, Jim now smells his breath for alcohol when Tyler comes home. Jim and Marsha are re-establishing their roles as parents and now are dealing with Tyler's Moreso issues.

If good parents with a normal "tough" child find themselves pushed to the limit, what about those children who have never bonded, whose attachment cycles have been disrupted, or who have been abused or shuffled from foster home to foster home during the first two years of life? What of those children born to teen mothers like Sherry? If the first two years were "not so good," the Moreso Theory tells us we'd better prepare for a difficult adolescence and a troubled adult life.

Section Three
(Everything I Do) I Do It For You[1]

As the song sung by Bryan Adams conveys, this is the attitude and intention adults need to maintain if they work with kids with the Love Disorder. Adults must be committed to the successful passage of the child through whatever endeavor brings them together. We must "get to them" – to their cores – and connect with them at that level if we are going to make a difference in their lives and reverse their disorder. But to reach them is to fight through their extraordinary defense structure, often without any positive reciprocation from them. This process represents the epitome of the Partnership Model. We enter into this partnership with these difficult kids because that is our calling – our passion – both to show them that their relationships with adults do not have to be painful and alienating, and to give them an opportunity to be successful in our common task and in our relationship. Within that partnership, everything that we do, we do it for them.

Chapter 9

What About DAT?

In the field of psychotherapy, attachment therapy is relatively new. One of several current interpretations and applications to the work being practiced around the world is Dynamic Attachment Therapy (DAT), as developed by my colleagues and me at the Human Passages Institute (HPI) in Lakewood, Colorado, (a suburb of Denver) since 1991. DAT is taking its place as another step in the evolution of understanding and treatment of Reactive Attachment Disorders in youth.

DAT is a strategic combination of applied attachment theory and more traditional psychotherapy and serves to treat some of the most resistant psychopathologies known to the mental health field. It has been designed to allow and help therapists understand and treat patients who have developed resistance to other treatment modalities and because of the typical failure of traditional treatment.

DAT is (D)ynamic because: 1) it is not static; it is a living, breathing, ever-changing explanation of the underlying emotional make-up that drives at-risk behavior. 2) It deals with the person on a deeper emotional level instead of a thinking, behavioral level. DAT continues to include (A)ttachment theory as it evolves and deals in both T)heory to promote understanding and (T)reatment to promote the changes necessary to dissolve the defeating behaviors. At HPI, we use DAT to encompass both understanding and treating youth with attachment disorders.

Dynamic Attachment Therapy is based upon two major premises: First, the quality of the mother-infant attachment, especially during the first two years of life, determines the quality of the capacity for the individual to form meaningful, lasting, reciprocal interpersonal relationships throughout a lifetime. Second, the pain, mistrust, and lack of safety that result from the disruption of the mother-infant bond promotes learned pathological responses as adaptations to those negative feelings.

Disruptions that result from the break in the mother-infant attachment can have many causal factors, ranging from the obvious – such as the primal wound of adoption, physical/sexual abuse, or severe neglect and abandonment – to the more subtle, and, therefore, more difficult-to-detect factors such as problematic genetics, poor pre-natal care, birth trauma, childhood illnesses or accidents, negligent daycare, ineffective parenting styles, etc. Any of these factors may result in the child not receiving the care he needs.

This breach of the ethological, social, and spiritual contract between parent and child causes what has been called "Basic Anxiety" – the child's feeling of being isolated and helpless in a potentially hostile world.[1] The discomfort the child experiences as a result of the incongruence between her needs and the extent to which those needs are met by the caregivers, primarily Mom, is the "Pain Gap." The wider the "gap," the more intense the pain – and the more imperative surviving the pain becomes. See Figure 5:

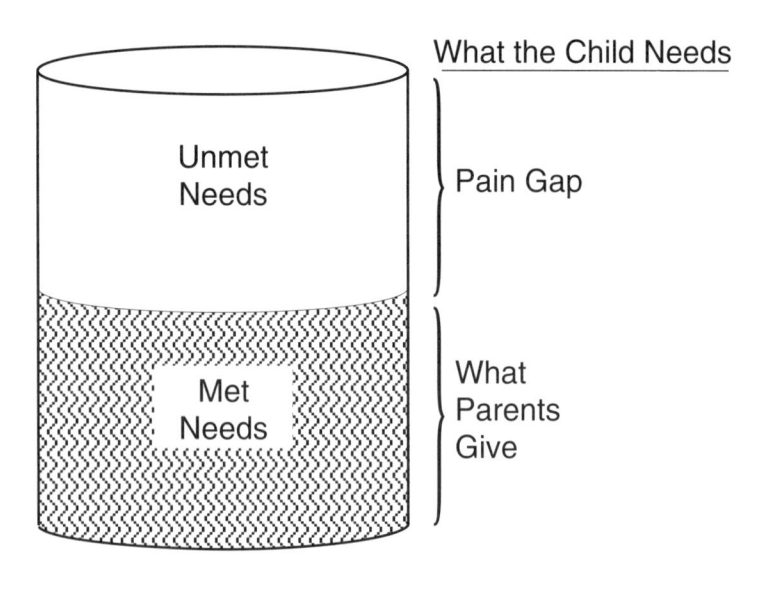

Figure 5

Even with the best of parenting, children's needs can't always be met; the extent that each child *suffers* from unmet needs is the degree to which the child must deal with the pain gap. This is the basis of the continuum we've been describing: all youth are at risk to some degree.

As neo-Freudian Karen Horney states, children who receive too little warmth and encouragement from their parents are especially prone to basic anxiety. Feeling more and more helpless and insecure as parents continue to neglect and intimidate them, anxious children begin to harbor deep feelings of resentment and anger toward parents. But the feeling cannot be expressed directly because the parents appear to be so big and powerful. Consequently, the child feels even greater levels of anxiety because of the surging hostile impulses within.[2]

What Horney has labeled "neurotic conflicts" can be traced to faulty interpersonal relationships in which hostility and basic anxiety make for the "alienation of an individual from his or her real self."[3] She states that the neurotic may use one of three different strategies for coping with inner conflict: "moving toward people, moving against people, or moving away from people."[4]

The term "neurosis" was coined by the Englishman William Cullen[5] and first used in his System of Nosology, 1769, in which he referred to disordered sensations of the nervous system. A more modern concept states that "neurotic symptoms are generally viewed as exaggerated defense mechanisms arising out of unconscious attempts to cope with internal conflicts and the anxiety they produce."[6] Neurotic people typically have trouble making and sustaining relationships and tend to be quite dependent and insecure.

The text *Abnormal Psychology and Modern Life* defines a "character disorder": "…characterized by faulty attitudes and personality trends which tend to manifest themselves in deviant or maladjusted behavior…"[7]

The Diagnostic and Statistical Manual of Mental Disorders (DSM-IV), which is the standard used in the field of mental health to measure diagnoses, states, "It is only when personality traits are inflexible and maladaptive and cause either significant impairment in social or occupational functioning or subjective distress that they constitute personality disorders. Some identifying traits:

1) Inadequate conscience development and lack of anxiety and guilt.
2) Irresponsible and impulsive behavior; low frustration tolerance.

3) Ability to put up a good front, project blame.
4) Reject authority, don't profit from experience.
5) Inability to maintain good relationships.[8]

Now, you could be saying, "Hey, I know someone like that," or even, "Hey, wait a minute, that sounds like me!" Certainly, we all exhibit some of these behaviors some of the time. The key word here is "some." The true character disorder exhibits most of these behaviors most of the time, and ironically, if you thought this sounded like you, you probably don't have a character disorder – since a true character disorder doesn't think he has a problem…which *is* the problem!

In his book *The Road Less Traveled,* M. Scott Peck says these two conditions, neurosis and character disorder, are disorders of responsibility. (I would add the idea that responsibility is the opposite of alienation.) He defines them succinctly and precisely: " The neurotic assumes too much responsibility; the person with the character disorder not enough."[9] He also says, "Few of us can escape being neurotic or character disordered to at least some degree (which is why essentially everyone can benefit from psychotherapy if he or she is seriously willing to participate in the process)."[10]

This is the same insightful argument raised by 14-year old Donald: "We all have problems,. What's normal?" I responded, using my best Orwellian logic, "Some of us are more 'normal' than others."

One of the points that Peck makes about character disorders is crucial: "Neurotics make themselves miserable; those with character disorders make everyone else miserable."[11] Also, the research is clear that, while counseling and therapy are effective with neurotics, the results are less than positive with character disorders.[12] This makes sense, because the person with a character disorder has difficulty accepting responsibility and is more likely to place blame elsewhere: "If it's not my fault, why should I seek help?" would be one of the character-disorder's lines of reasoning.

I interpret Horney and Peck's theories as essentially identifying the same problems. The neurotic may "move toward people" by being clingy, manipulative, or enabling; while the character-disorder may isolate and "move away" to avoid conflict or to avoid being dependent. Or, he may "move against" and attack before he is attacked. I would trace the conflict back to the disrupted attachment cycle and the resulting pain gap.

This takes us back to our continuum. I believe that we are talking about a continuum of difference of attachment disruptions in kids, as opposed to differences of kind of kids. It's not a matter of there being attached kids and unattached kids. I don't think that's the case. If there have been completely unattached kids, they are dead or in jail. I firmly believe that no parenting completely satisfies the child's needs 100 percent of the time *or* fulfills the attachment cycle to the extent that there is not a disruption or a tinge of mistrust.

So, we've moved from what is depicted in Figure 6:

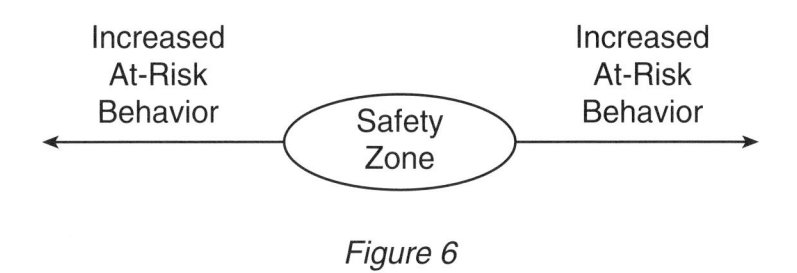

Figure 6

to what is shown in Figure 7:

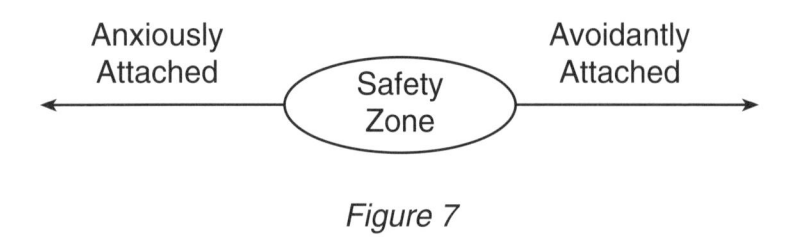

```
Anxiously                           Avoidantly
Attached        ( Safety Zone )     Attached
<---------------              ---------------->
```

Figure 7

to what is represented in Figure 8:

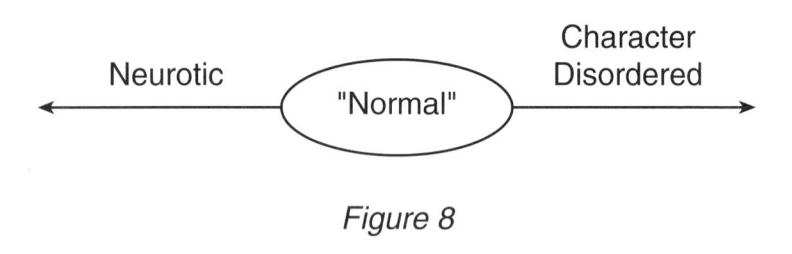

```
                                    Character
Neurotic        ( "Normal" )        Disordered
<---------------            ------------------>
```

Figure 8

We are discussing the same dynamics just named by different theories. Let's combine them to see the overview. See Figure 9:

56

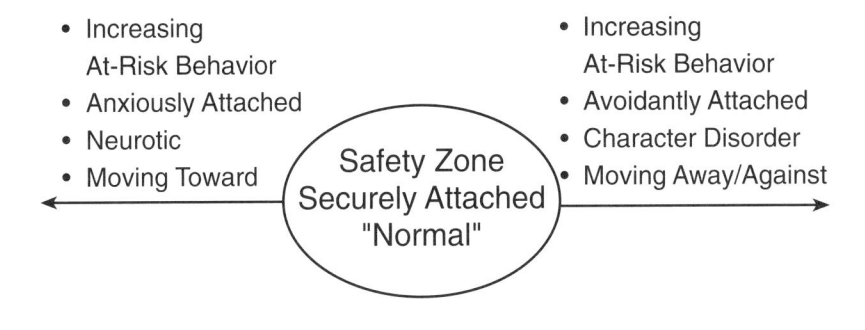

- Increasing At-Risk Behavior
- Anxiously Attached
- Neurotic
- Moving Toward

Safety Zone
Securely Attached
"Normal"

- Increasing At-Risk Behavior
- Avoidantly Attached
- Character Disorder
- Moving Away/Against

Figure 9

Each of these continuums is interchangeable.

DAT also recognizes that breaks in the successful completion of the attachment cycle can also be generated from within the dynamics of the child herself. There are three ways in which she can break the cycle:

1. She experiences a need but *cannot* (as in "is unable") express the need. (For example, a baby experiencing a chronic inner ear infection is not able to articulate the problem.) Or, she experiences a need but *will not* express it – a choice made that probably indicates resistance to re-experiencing the pain of some earlier life trauma. (For example, a verbal 6-year-old with an earache refuses to express her need because she fears the shots she may have to get for treatment.) See Figure 10:

The Attachment Cycle

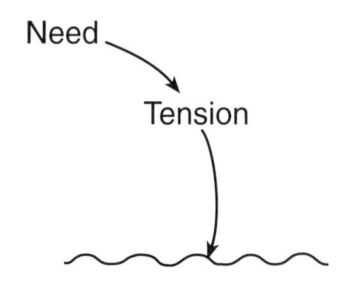

Need ↘
　　Tension

The child *cannot* or *will not* express the need. The cycle is broken, the need goes unmet, and the child remains needy and in a state of tension. There is no trust or safety.

Figure 10

2. Because of previous breaks in the attachment cycle, the child develops protective defenses and may express her needs in a crooked/distorted/coded fashion such that the caregiver cannot recognize the true need and, consequently, doesn't intervene. (A teenage girl may ask you to go shopping when what she really wants is to discuss a serious problem.) See Figure 11:

The Attachment Cycle

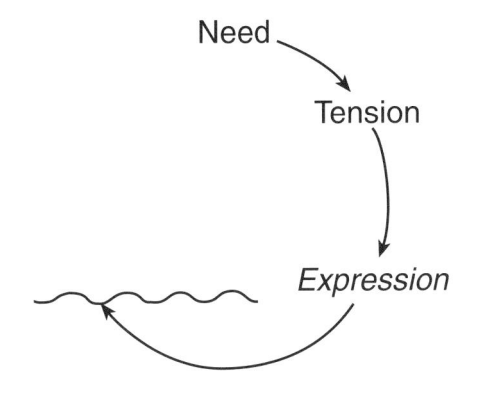

Need → Tension → Expression → (cycle back)

The need is expressed, but it is distorted/coded, and the parent doesn't intervene. Again, the need goes unmet, and the child remains needy and in tension with no trust or safety.

Figure 11

3. The child is so strongly defended and resistant to the caregiver that he refuses (consciously or unconsciously) to accept the parental intervention meant to address his need. We identify this dynamic as the child *cannot* (as "in not able to") give or receive love because of his intense defense structure. (For example, a child will sabotage [consciously or unconsciously] his birthday party or special outing because he can't accept the love [good times] created by the caregiver.) See Figure 12:

The Attachment Cycle

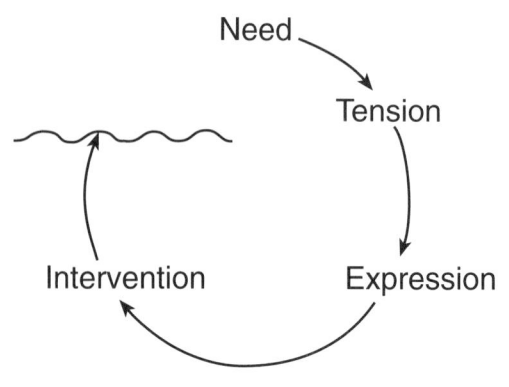

Need → Tension → Expression → Intervention (cycle)

The need is expressed, and the parent intervenes – but the child resists the intervention. The need goes unmet, the child remains needy and in tension with no trust or safety.

Figure 12

We often hear from the parents of attachment-disrupted children, "Our child refuses our love," or, "We continually give our child love and work hard to meet her needs, but nothing ever seems to make a difference to her." It is very important to note here that parents and caregivers must keep the perspective that the child *can't* give or receive love – this awareness will help the adults keep room in their hearts for compassion for the child. It will also allow the parent to "hang in there" with the child and continue to work on her problem. Parents who hold the perspective that the child *won't* give or receive love or accept parental interventions tend to personalize this dynamic, feel angry at the child, and get burned out sooner.

The bottom line is that breaks in healthy attachment (attachment cycle disruptions) can come from several sources – as well as be complicated by continued breaks because of the inner dynamics of the parent-child relationship. These breaks *will be as intense and as pervasive as the sum total of the original trauma plus the consequent complications of the parent-child dynamics.* All of this impacts the child in the following ways:

1. The child remains "needy."
2. He remains in a state of tension.
3. She feels the pain of betrayal.
4. He feels alienated and mistrusts the world in general and parents in particular.
5. She feels unsafe and unnurtured.
6. He fails to thrive.
7. She becomes resistant to discipline and parenting.
8. He develops attitudes and strategies geared to gain distance from the mistrusted adults.

The various applications of this defense structure develop into the previously mentioned diagnostic psychopathologies. While it is important to diagnose the problem, too often, I see children who are "stuck," usually because the diagnosis receives all the attention. Ironically, the child becomes secondary. We must remember the breaks the child experienced in the attachment cycle – and that diagnoses are basically labels we put on the coping mechanisms of how kids deal with these difficulties (more about diagnoses in the next section).

The goal of DAT is to heal the early life trauma (including the breach of the bonding contract). This healing can take place only after the defense structure is explored and restructured so that the patient has the ability to attach effectively in healthy, reciprocal relationships. Only then can compassion, love, and forgiveness be accepted rather than distorted or denied. Accomplishing this goal is not easy. It takes a lot of work, and it does not happen overnight. It also implies the presence of another person – a caregiver – in the child's life. Within the DAT model, we at HPI train parents to enter into a "special relationship" with the child – not to be only a parent but a *partner* as well. When this special relationship occurs, we believe we are on a positive, direct path for the child to experience several desirable outcomes:

1. Healing of early life trauma.
2. Establishment of positive interpersonal experiences between the parents/other adults and the child.
3. Increasing her opportunity to attach in healthy, reciprocal relationships.
4. Increasing his sense of self-regard.
5. Increasing her sense of safety and trust in the world.
6. Decreasing his anxiety and "neediness."
7. Decreasing her psychopathological symptoms.

Chapter 10

Partnership: The Special Glue

"Love is the glue that holds the world together." This quote was sent home to me from my son's first grade teacher as his answer to the question, "What do you think love is?" I was amazed at his insight and ability to abstract at such an age. But it just shows that kids know about these things. Kids (especially young ones) and animals know – or have a sense – of what is safe, what is important, what they need to do to be loved, and who can or can't provide these things.

The glue that holds Dynamic Attachment Therapy together is "partnership." Everything we do with kids at HPI is done out of the appropriateness of our adult relationship to them. From exchanging a hug to doing the dishes together to pushing through a therapeutic issue, the relationship itself dictates the degree of interaction, intimacy, and intervention used by the adult.

The concept of partnership transcends that of relationship. We are born into certain relationships, i.e., mother-daughter, brother-sister, uncle-nephew, etc. And society makes available to us (and defines for us) certain other relationships as we increase our social interaction, i.e., teacher-student, employer-employee, and even husband-wife. Being in partnership means to consciously and purposefully enter into an arrangement by contract to pursue a mutual endeavor. This is exactly what two people are doing, for example, when one asks the other to dance and the other accepts. We call them dance partners.

Most relationships stay at that level. There is no mutually agreed-upon goal, no purpose, and often no specific task. They simply exist in that relationship, whatever that means to each of them.

However, we realize that some relationships, when entered into with an intention to partner, become something more. They become a partnership – which means they are proactively seeking mutually agreed-upon, negotiated goals. Moreover, partnership also implies that each person has a commitment to the other. At a minimum, that commitment is to see the task through to its end while honoring each person's responsibility to the other.

But at its fullest and most significant, a partnership is the intention of *knowing the value of each other as human beings;* to bring forward in each other the worthwhile individual characteristics that compose human dignity. It is the intention of seizing the opportunity to actualize human potential. It is seizing the opportunity to grow within the struggle of the fulfillment of the partnership.

The purpose of being in partnership is to remind us all that there is an immutable and desirable quality of interaction that can guide human relationships. When people are in partnership, they have the opportunity to view and treat each other this way. They have moved from relationship (unconsciously accepting role expectations) to true partnership (acting according to these humanistic attitudes and intentions).

Every Human Core

For human beings to enhance the quality of their interactions through partnership, it is a good idea to know more about human beings as individuals first. Let's take a closer look at human individuality.

At Human Passages Institute (HPI), within the scope of the DAT model, we operate on the premise that people embody two groups of qualities: universal (undifferentiated) and personal (differentiated). The first set are those human qualities that would be considered *universal;* people are *undifferentiated* by them. In other words, we recognize qualities that we all have, and because we all have them, our individuality cannot be distinguished.

In philosophy, we are talking about the very nature – the qualities – that make humans...well, human. In theology, we are describing what would be considered the human spirit–again, the essence of human life. Human essence is different than the essence of animals, fruit, or tennis balls. Each group has a unique set of qualities that contribute to its existence as that group. No one is in the group who doesn't have those qualities (because then, they would be something else.)

So, what are these traits that make us human? Philosophers and theologians have been arguing this forever. But I think the more salient points for this discussion are that all humans have the capacity for knowledge (intellect), choice (free will), love (caring attachments), aesthetics (appreciation for truth, goodness, and beauty), and responsibility (awareness of and accountability for human potential).

Let's chart this. (You can see I like charts...)

Take these undifferentiated qualities that we all have and value as worthwhile and put them on a continuum: See Figure 13:

More   Less

|————————————————————————|

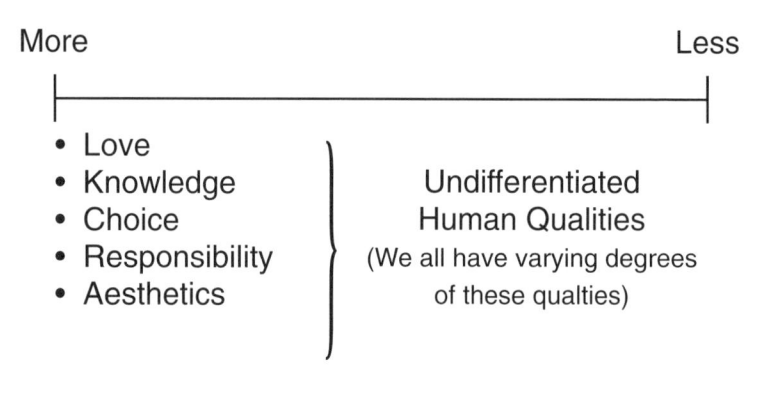

- Love
- Knowledge
- Choice
- Responsibility
- Aesthetics

} Undifferentiated Human Qualities
(We all have varying degrees of these qualties)

Figure 13

We all have various degrees of these traits. Now put the continuum into a circle: See Figure 14:

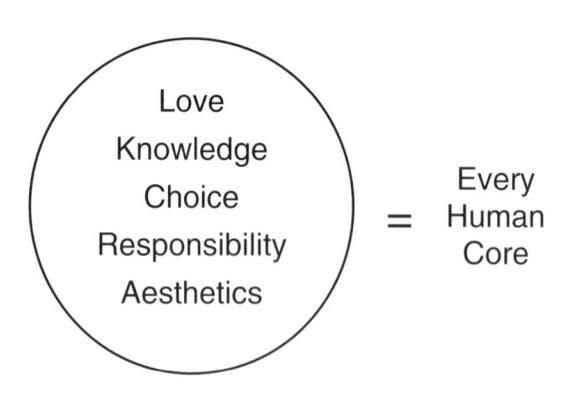

(Love
Knowledge
Choice
Responsibility
Aesthetics) = Every Human Core

Figure 14

This essentially becomes the core of each human being. We spiritual folks would add that the spirit of God also resides within this core – which also makes us "Children of God." The core of each human is then essential, pure, valuable, and worth nurturing. A biblical paraphrase would read, "God made man in his own image and saw that it was good; then he made woman and saw it was fantastic!" The core is the essence of human spirit, shared by *all* humans.

Every known culture presently and throughout history has a term or concept for the human core the way we are describing it here. The Chinese, for example, talk of the essential inner part of man that contains the oneness of all being. They call it *"Li."* So, each of us has a *"Li"* or a center that contains the themes common to all Being.

Also, like so many cultures that have one word for both hello and good-bye (*"Aloha"* in Hawaiian, *"Shalom"* in Hebrew), the Hindus have the term *"Namaste,"* which is used as a greeting or parting comment. The broader meaning encompasses the concept:

I recognize that within you there is a place where the entire universe resides; when you are in that place in you and I am in that place in me, we are one.

Namaste is a very special message. When spoken, it acknowledges recognition of a connection between the cores of two people.

Distancing Human Qualities

As humans, however, we are not perfect at residing completely within our cores. We have taken on the trappings of being human – that is, we have developed qualities that *differentiate* us from our core – and from one another.

Charted, there would be continuums of each quality (I like continuums): See Figure 15:

```
More                    Less  ⎫  • Feelings
├──  ──  ──  ──  ──┤          ⎬  • Job
   Differentiated Human Qualities  • Political Beliefs
                              ⎭  • Hobbies
                                 • etc.
```

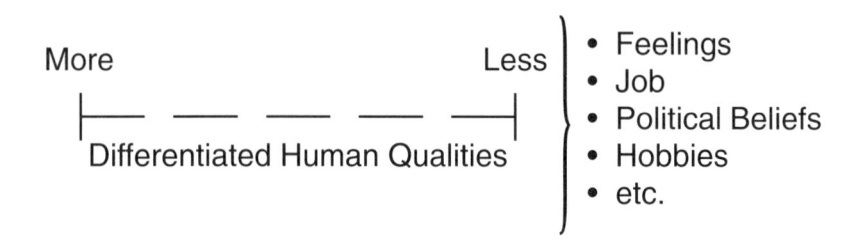

Figure 15

The line is perforated because some of us have these qualities to greater or lesser degrees. The smaller the spaces and the thicker the lines, the more predominant the quality in any one person. See Figure 16:

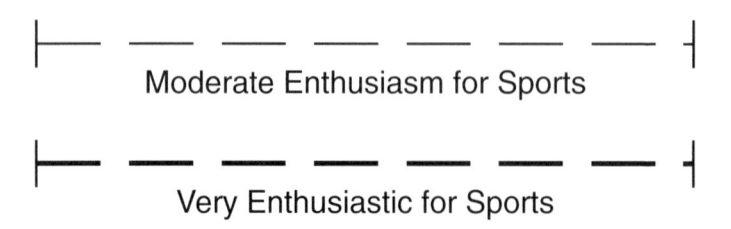

```
├──  ──  ──  ──  ──  ──  ──┤
      Moderate Enthusiasm for Sports

├──  ──  ──  ──  ──  ──  ──┤
       Very Enthusiastic for Sports
```

Figure 16

Someone who is driven (obsessed) with sports – knows all the scores, watches all the games, and feels guilty when he misses an event – would look like this: See Figure 17:

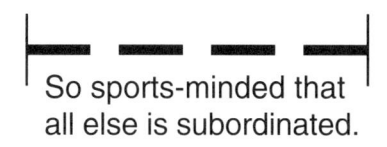

|— — — —|
So sports-minded that
all else is subordinated.

Figure 17

Our second group of human qualities are *personal* because they help define each of us as the unique person we are. We all have feelings, jobs, political beliefs, hobbies, etc., that distinguish us from others. (By the way, these are all distancing phenomena because, by definition, they are meant to *separate* us from one another.) Now, wrap these many continuums (one continuum for each trait) into a circle and a person's personal traits would look like Figure 18:

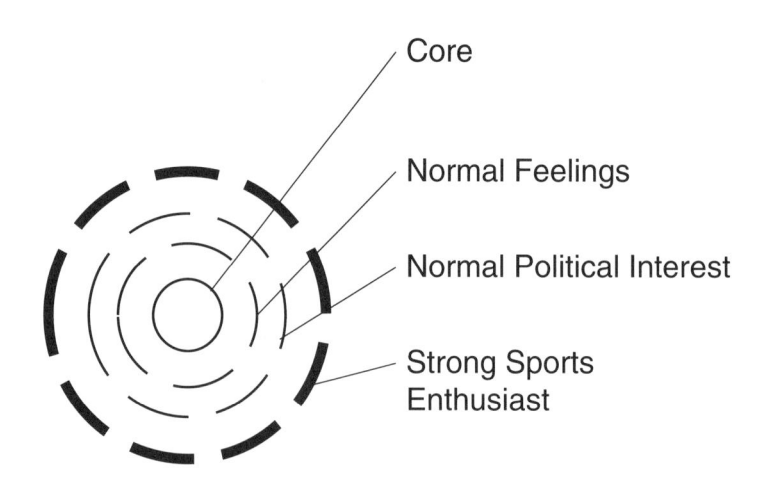

- Core
- Normal Feelings
- Normal Political Interest
- Strong Sports Enthusiast

Figure 18

The more layers, the harder it is to find the person's core. The more "trappings" or issues a person possesses, the more difficult it is for her to relate and be "related to" by others. See Figure 19:

How do we get into this person?
She looks and acts like a maze.

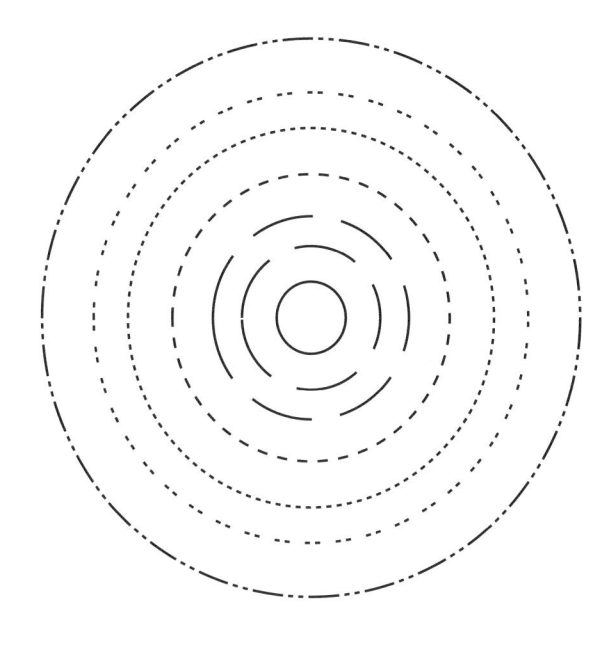

Figure 19

Also, the stronger the trait, the more difficult it is to get into the personality and, eventually, to the core. Therefore, intensity is also a factor as to whether she is so entrenched with any particular issue that her core is difficult to access. See Figure 20:

Core

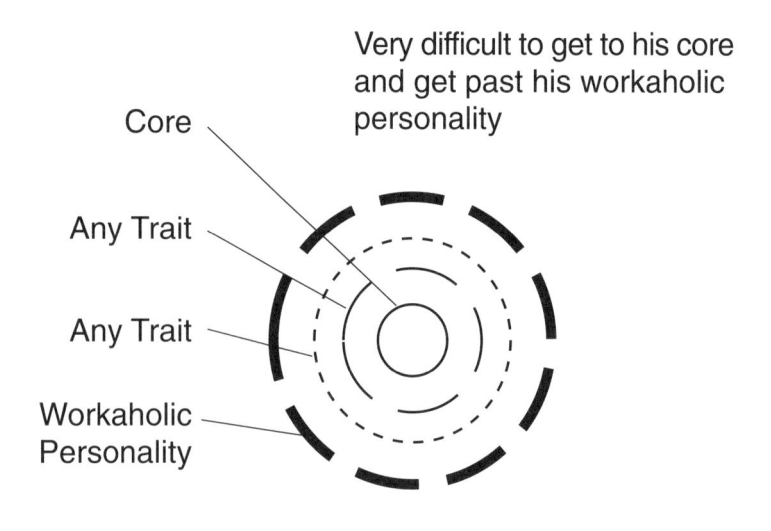

Very difficult to get to his core and get past his workaholic personality

Any Trait

Any Trait

Workaholic Personality

Figure 20

An infinite number of these qualities define uniqueness; but let's discuss a few that are necessary in order for us to understand our children and their issues.

So many of the kids we work with have poor attachment histories. That means that they have had some experiences that have become barriers to their ability to form healthy, caring attachments. Remember to keep in mind that these experiences can include physical/emotional/sexual abuse, severe neglect, abandonment, multiple placements, medical conditions, birth trauma, death of (or separation from) caregivers, etc.

The feelings that result from these breaks in attachment can be considered the "Pain Gap" discussed earlier – and it is this Pain Gap that *perceptually* needs to be defended. The defense structure can be simple or elaborate, depending on the perceived need of the individual.

The earlier in life that the trauma occurs, the more fragile the child, the more *primal* the feelings, the more primitive the response, and the more desperate the need to defend *because she perceives it as a life-or-death situation.* When trauma occurs in a child's life, it triggers the perception that her life is in danger. The younger she is, the more vulnerable and sensitive she is to this perception. Her natural response to trauma is to use attachment as a coping device. If it is not available on an affective or emotional level to protect her, she fears that her life is in danger – her *self* is in danger.

Early attachments are established at the level of survival. Bowlby believed that an infant has an internal attachment system – and that, as each attachment is formed, the internal system is adapted with each experience.[1] This translates into the idea that we *all* have an attachment "style" that provides the clues to how, why, and when we seek proximity to people we trust in order to gain comfort.

The infant who has experienced trauma and does not have solid attachments to use as coping devices must seek other strategies to protect against the threat of annihilation. Those early strategies form the basis of the child's defense structure.

The Layers of the Defense Structure

Like a tree growing its rings from the inside out, the defense structure also develops in layers beginning at the core. Each layer is an additional system of defense intended to protect the tender center. Although there could be countless layers of defenses for any and all of us, we understand and examine the defense structure relevant to the child's attachment issues. By using DAT, we group the defensive structure into four main layers that cover and protect a person's core. They are listed from the inside outwardly:

1. **Primal Negative Feelings**: Although the child outwardly exhibits some configuration of defeating behaviors – such as a hostile, angry attitude, substance abuse, eating disorders, and self-mutilation – DAT postulates that there is a deep-seated root for these feelings. Because of the absence of a healthy attachment system that would allow the child to cope successfully, she feels that her very existence is being threatened. Survival is the most basic and primal urge or instinct within us. Therefore, the threat of annihilation triggers the deepest and most intense feelings known to any human being: the child *experiences* incredible depths of feeling sad, mad, and scared.

    At HPI, we know not just from the theory but from our clinical experience that, at that depth of sadness, there is an intense *despair* that renders the child hopeless and helpless to resolve the trauma of his impending annihilation (see Figure 21). The *rage* that accompanies the depth of anger looks like what we call "killing feelings" – and that is what he is actually experiencing. He is essentially expressing, "I am so full of rage (about feeling that my life is in jeopardy) that I could kill someone – or someone will have to kill me to stop me" (Figure 21). And a debilitating sense of *terror* exists at the depth of fear or feeling scared. I firmly believe that it is this sense of terror that keeps most of the attachment-disrupted children stuck in their defensive structure (Figure 21). Most of us cannot even imagine what it is like for a child to live day-to-day carrying this kind of emotional anvil around with him.

Surface feelings of sad, mad and scared actually are experienced at their deepest level as the **primal negative feelings** of *despair, rage* and *terror.*

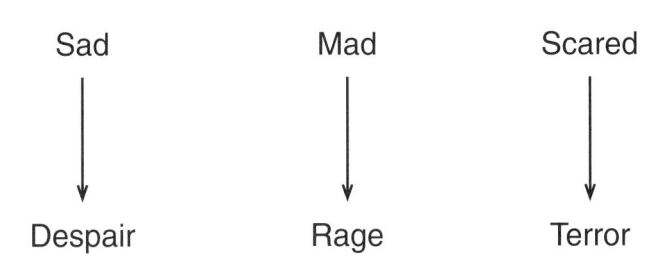

```
  Sad           Mad          Scared
   ↓             ↓             ↓
 Despair        Rage          Terror
```

Figure 21

At this first level of defense, these intense feelings are real – yet raw and unconscious. And, like a foreign object introjected into the personality, they are pervasive and overwhelming.

2. **Self-Concept**: The formation of the defense structure occurs immediately following the attachment breaks. As this is happening, the child develops a degree of hyper-vigilance and preoccupation with the parental relationship. That is, she becomes focused solely on the parent as the answer for her needs being met. This dynamic, then, prohibits her from using the relationship (attachment) as a secure base from which she can explore the world and keeps her energy and focus on achieving proximity with a caregiver who is not meeting her needs. Instead of a true attachment within which both people are developing their human potential, the infant's misplaced focus prevents her from participating in the

healthy development of separation-individuation. She holds onto a projective identification with the parent and, therefore, isn't free to develop her sense of *self*. She is now "caught" in the trap of not knowing who she is or who she is in relation to this parent or caregiver. This trap affects her self-concept in several ways:

    A. She will continually accept the values of the caregiver as her own – which means that she becomes severely handicapped in her quest to develop her own values.
    B. She will remain defended and confused about herself and will continue to be unable to separate and individuate.
    C. She will typically blame herself for the failure of the attachment and perceive the caregiver as loving and available – whether that perception is accurate or not.
    D. The child will spend excessive energy trying to "win the love" (in an attempt to fix what's broken) of the unavailable (in her eyes) caregiver by engaging in a "trial-and-error" process of pleasing behaviors.

Each of these results keeps the child from participating in the normal, natural process of separation-individuation that leads to the development of a healthy self-concept.

3. **Development of Conscience**: Because the child is (a) preoccupied with simply surviving, (b) busy fighting off the devastating primal feelings of annihilation, and (c) virtually void of the values, attitudes, and beliefs that compose a healthy self-concept, he lacks both the information and the desire (the ego strength) to process the rightness and wrongness of his behavior. Without the

frame of reference of a healthy sense of self, he will not develop the inner controls necessary to guide him in his ethical behavior. Regardless of how accurate or inaccurate, clearly defined or vague a child's frame of reference may be, it provides his only basis for evaluating new experiences and coping with the world. As a consequence, the child *tends to defend his existing faulty assumptions of self and the world and proceed to interact with the world seemingly without regard to what is right or wrong* – or the cost to himself or others – instead of behaving in ways that might actually help him get his immediate needs met.

4. **Presenting Behaviors**: The outer ring of the defense structure could be referred to as "What you see is what you get." It consists of how the child looks, acts, and presents herself to the world. Of course, there is so much more to her than what she is able to show on the surface. Nevertheless, invariably, the attachment-disrupted child presents herself, in various degrees, as rooted in a predictable range of defeating behaviors. These are the maladaptive behaviors she has learned as the result of her "trial-and-error" strategy to get what she needs from her caregivers and the world. The presenting behaviors are learned pathology to defend against the pain of the broken attachments and the resulting Pain Gap (as discussed earlier).

The range of presenting behaviors is wide but quite predictable. Some kids present as depressed, some as anxious, some as calloused, angry, superficial, charming, fun or witty, street-smart, detached, etc. Yet, the behaviors that surface from these "life stances" are all meant to defend the child's core by basically controlling the closeness (or distance) of relationships – especially in relationships with caregivers – or later, anyone with whom the person is vulnerable emotionally.

At HPI, we make assessments of these four components of the defense structure for each child we treat. This is done so that we can develop a "map" of where we need to go in therapy, as well as attempting to detect which "in-roads" we may take to get to the child's core as soon as possible. DAT is based on the premise that connecting to the child's core will provide him with the hope and perception that there *are* caregivers in the world who are able and willing to enter into a partnership with him. The DAT map of the defense structure generically looks like Figure 22:

Core
#1 Primal Negative Emotions
#2 Poor Self – Concept
#3 Lack of Conscience Development
#4 Presenting Behaviors

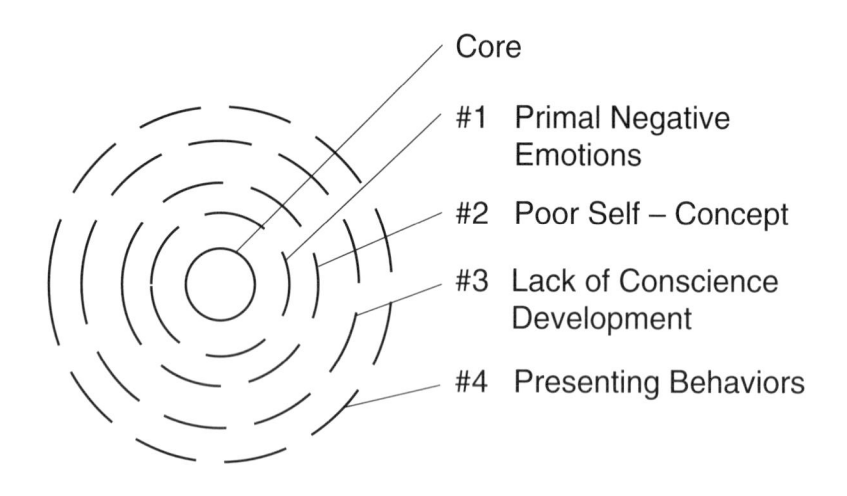

Figure 22

Now, let us examine a specific example of a child with attachment issues and chart her defense structure.

(See Figure 23.) She presents as tough in each area but especially shows little conscience-development, has a very weak self-concept, and is stuck in her primary emotions.

> This would be someone who acts tough in whatever way (presenting behaviors) but shows little conscience, has very weak self-esteem, and is stuck in her primary emotions.

Core
#1 Primal Negative Emotions
#2 Poor Self-Concept
#3 Lack of Conscience Development
#4 Presenting Behaviors

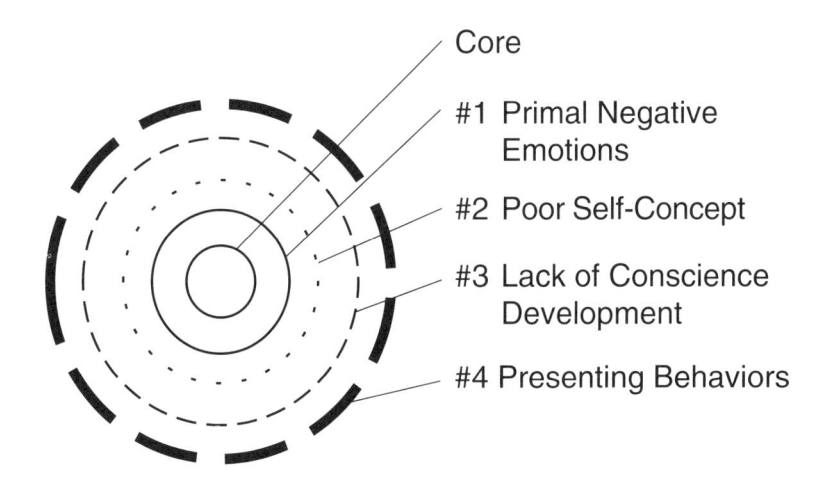

Figure 23

She is so insulated or thickly defended that her real core is completely covered. It *seems* that her apparent core is her defensiveness, anger, and pain (primal in nature). It *appears* as though she has no worthwhile core – only hostile, negative emotions. However, we know that this is not the case – this is not all there is to this child. We insist that we must penetrate this defense structure and find the "real" core of the individual.

How does anyone relate to such a damaged, protected kid, let alone treat him in therapy? This challenge is compounded because we now have two people – child and therapist (two sets of differentiated and undifferentiated human qualities) – trying to understand one another and interact.

At best, it is difficult to relate on each of the outer layers – let alone to actually reach each other at the core level (which is my definition of intimacy). Look how difficult it is to reach a core when the child is so thickly insulated and the adult is not: See Figure 24:

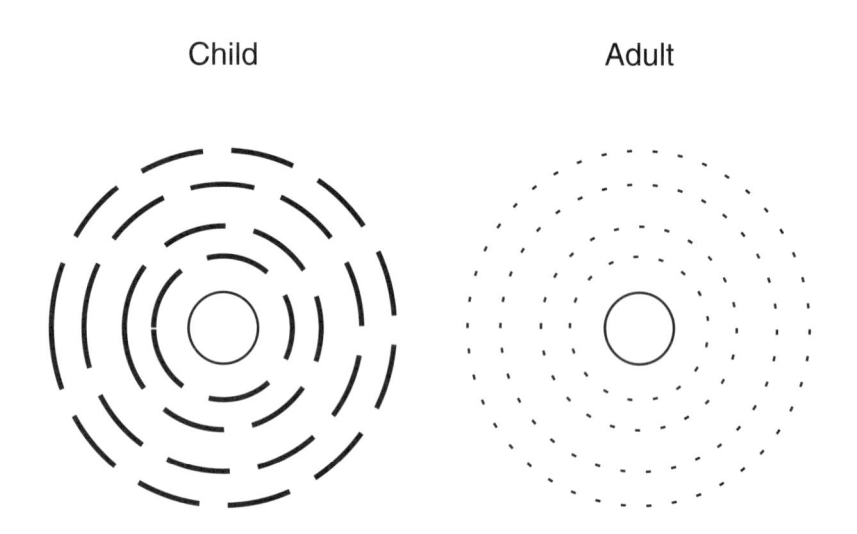

Child   Adult

Figure 24

As can be seen, the adult is very balanced in her differentiated traits and her core can be readily accessed. But the child is thickly defended, and approaching his core will be most difficult. Therefore, the relationship itself will be challenging to form and maintain at any level of depth.

Object Relations, a school of psychology and one of the three branches that contribute to attachment theory, states that children with attachment issues attempt to control the distance of their adult-child relationship[2]. This is a result of their perception that closeness is threatening to their safety and freedom to be an individual. They attempt this control in four ways:

1. They keep themselves moving in and out of closeness – both as a conscious decision and as a kind of unconscious automatic manipulation.
2. When that can't happen, they put barriers between themselves and the adult, such as closed doors, staying out late, stereo headphones, and other distancing phenomena.
3. They try to get the adult to move away by acting obnoxious, lying, stealing, acting aggressively, etc.
4. They insulate themselves; that is, they make their defenses internally thicker and stronger so that no one can get in.

They want the adult kept on a shelf as an object so that she's there if they want her (a ride to the mall) – and *not* there if they don't want her to be. So they "use" the object when desirable and push it away back on the shelf when not desirable.

In society, we often talk of the "layers" of people and relationships. We have to "get to the bottom" of his problems; the "tip of the tongue;" I mean it "from the bottom of my heart;" "hard-core" addict; she's so "superficial and phony;" we're in the "middle" of a relationship, etc.

So it is with DAT. We want to get to a kid's core as soon as possible. But, too often, we have to work through all of the issues and defense structures before that can happen. We have a pretty good map of what those layers look like and how to get through them; however, we know first and foremost that it is the *partnership* itself that drives the direction and speed of that movement. It is the partnership that ultimately determines the degree of success.

Therefore, all of the parenting techniques and therapeutic interventions that we promote are done within the context of partnership. How far its elasticity will stretch is always a consideration.

Thus, forming, evaluating, and working within the partnership is an important component of DAT. The next section will present the entire model – that is, partnering with the attachment-disrupted kids we work with at HPI.

Chapter 11

The Partnership Model of Discipline

We have found that practicing the partnership model has had profoundly positive results in breaking through these thick layers of defense and getting to the core of the child. Once this breakthrough can happen, he is more open to giving and receiving love, care, and nurture. This increase in his openness to receiving helps him develop the trust and safety necessary for him to be in his truth about expressing needs and recognizing the needs of others.

This model is designed for adults who deal with children. At Human Passages Institute, we believe that, in a sense, these children pass *through* us. We have them for whatever period of time that our common tasks bind us together, whether we are their fourth-grade teacher, their case worker, their Girl Scout leader, their therapist, their foster parent, or even their natural parent. We have that one window of opportunity to assist them in a successful passage through our territory. As Kahlil Gibran wrote so eloquently in *The Prophet:*

> Your children are not your children.
> They are the sons and daughters
>   of Life's longing for itself.
> They come through you
>   but not from you.
> And though they are with you,
>   yet they belong not to you.

> You may give them your love
> > but not your thoughts.
> You may house their bodies
> > but not their souls...
> You may strive to be like them,
> > but seek not to make them like you...[1]

The partnership involves both participants (the adult and the child) committing to the successful passage of the child through the endeavor that brings them together. It is not a partnership of equal say – but it *is* a partnership of equal commitment to the relationship itself, while both struggle with the child's passage.

The Two Goals of the Partnership Model

The Primary Goal: Engage the child in the process of healthy, productive partnering, such that the relationship itself becomes the object of the process.

The Secondary Goal: Train the child in the task that brings you together and assist in her passage through it.

Both goals are crucial for successful relationships and successful passages by the child. We are simply stressing that the quality of the bond – the relationship itself – is more important than the task that brings them together (scouting, fifth grade, etc.). The quality of the relationship dictates the activities that are either appropriate or not between the adult and the child.

Section Four
The More I Know You...The More I Love You

It is true and necessary! The more we know about each child, the Love Disorder and about ourselves partnering with our children whose ability to form healthy attachments has been disrupted, the more prepared and effective we will be. These kids are difficult to understand, difficult to reach, and difficult to partner with. Yet, equipping ourselves with knowledge, healthy energy, and a "decoder ring" helps us "translate" their defeating behavior and crooked messages (and underlying feelings) into an understanding of them and their disorder that allows us to operate from true compassion. So, truly, the more we know them...the move we love them.

Chapter 12

Prerequisites For Effective Partnering In Discipline

Since this model focuses on the contribution made by each participant, the adult is challenged to enter the partnership as healthy, knowledgeable, and as skilled as necessary. Of course, skill and wisdom in interventions with children are valuable, but there is much to say about the preparation that could eliminate or minimize difficulties.

For effective partnering in discipline, the adult needs to be prepared. Although parents are not their child's therapist, much of what they do is therapeutic. Participating in the partnership model and possessing the necessary prerequisites can certainly make the parents "professional partners."

The Partnership Model is a parenting model even though the material is presented in language that designates a professional as the adult partner. It is intended for parents to use to enhance their ability and the quality of their children's attachments to them. We believe this model is effective in working with children in a variety of adult-child relationships. It is being offered for parents of attachment-disrupted kids so they can begin to understand and appreciate the complexity of what's going on between them and their child – and become more prepared to participate with an attachment therapist at whatever time is appropriate.

The following prerequisites are necessary to have in place before the adult even meets the child (partner) for the first time. The adult must know, understand, and believe certain things about herself, the child, and the attachment disorder itself.

About You

1. Be healthy. Develop a clean (free from emotional baggage), balanced disposition. Have interest, excitement, and openness to learning about yourself and the child. Try not to be defended or closed to ideas or negotiating, hooked into his issues, or too tired to use good judgment.
2. Be knowledgeable and skilled in your content area of the child's passage, whether it is as her teacher, coach, parent, social worker, therapist, scout leader, etc.
3. Have a working knowledge of the Partnership Model.
4. Have good boundaries. Partnering does not imply violation of boundaries. It is essential for the adult partner to maintain a sense of self; that is, know and honor your limitations of time, energy, and expertise. Keep personal issues in check, and know the rights and responsibilities of the role you are in. Do not cross over; neither should you allow the child to cross over into impropriety.
5. Be honest and live in truth both for you and for the child. Don't "set up" or trap him for the purpose of teaching him a lesson.
6. Make sure that your humor never hurts others.

About the Child

1. Believe that each child who comes to you is valuable and worthwhile.
2. Understand that each child has legitimate needs and a history of various degrees of conditions (disruptions to the attachment cycle) that make her easier ← → or more difficult to partner with.

3. Have a working knowledge of the causal conditions that disrupt healthy attachment. We often do not know exactly what those causal factors are; neither do we always *need* to know in order to effectively partner with the child. But the following conditions must be understood and addressed to more effectively partner with children:

   A. Prenatal conditions:
      - wanted or unwanted pregnancy
      - hormonal distribution
      - sensory or stimulation difficulties
      - proper nutrition
      - Fetal Alcohol Syndrome, nicotine, caffeine, other substance abuse
      - physical trauma, birth defects
      - birth trauma
   B. Parenting conditions:
      - neglectful parenting, prolonged separation from caregiver
      - anxious or uncomfortable caregivers
      - overly rigid caregivers
      - unpredictable care
      - poor, unskilled parenting styles
   C. Traumatic conditions:
      - illness, accidents
      - abuse, neglect, abandonment
      - family problems, i.e., alcoholism, death of family member, divorce
      - adoption, multiple placements, moving the residence.

4. Be able to decode the defeating behaviors.

   This can be done by understanding the underlying feeling states the child experiences as a result of early life trauma. Ironically, when a child acts out, it is sometimes a relief, since it is then easier to identify and clarify the "apparent" problem or the circumstances that precipitated the behavior.

What is invariably more complex is getting to and dealing with the core issue. The unpleasant coping behaviors the child has developed often mask his true feelings – which creates exactly what he thinks he wants: distance from the adult, and, therefore, protection from the pain of not getting his needs met. These underlying feeling states are, especially: fear/rage, sadness/loss, loss of trust, need to self-parent, and reversed behavior patterns.

Fear/Rage

This is the basis for the underlying feeling states. While it is most often repressed and defended, it is intense because it is representative of the primitive rage and fear the child felt as an infant. It becomes a question of survival for her – a response to trust betrayed. Her response feels like she must: kill (rage), for the betrayal of trust; and/or be killed (fear), in which she will fail to survive because of unmet needs.

Because of this "kill-or-be-killed" perception, she covers the fear/rage, seeing its expression as another threat to survival.

Sadness/Loss

This feeling is also brought to the extreme and usually remains repressed and unresolved. The child irrationally and unconsciously concludes that any chance of reconciliation with the adult is lost. He develops a sense of helplessness and/or hopelessness and concludes that he is not worthwhile enough to be cared for or deserving of affection. Once again, he fears that the expression of these feelings will eliminate any chance of righting past wrongs and regaining his relationship with the adult.

Loss of Trust

The child feels alienated from the adult because her needs have not been met at specific points that were vital to her healthy development. This loss of trust manifests as conscious anger, a surface emotion that drives responses of opposition, defiance, aggression, or passive aggression.

Need to Self-Parent

The child knows that it is neither safe nor productive to act on the fear/rage feelings. In addition, it is important to recognize that his living in a state of hopelessness and/or helplessness keeps his needs unmet. Thus, he becomes "self-parenting" and develops strategies to meet his own needs. This results in his *resistance* to closeness and discipline and his compulsive *manipulation* of others and his environment.

Reversed Behavior Patterns

Normal attachment responses to negative behaviors lose their attractiveness or reinforcing quality. The attachment-disrupted child concludes something akin to: "When I misbehave, people send me away, fight with me, are unhappy, and don't get close. That is what I want. I'm being bad because closeness causes feelings I don't want to deal with. I've learned that people stop demanding compliance and leave me alone when I act like a jerk."

Thus, behaviors that drive people away or lessen their demands are reinforced. The reinforcement of negative behaviors lead to a "learned pathology."

Some of the typical behavior patterns we see every day are:

- Withdrawal from interaction
- Not affectionate on parents' terms
- Word games ("I didn't hit him, I just pushed him real hard with my fist")
- Accident prone
- Crazy lying (lying when the truth would make more sense)
- Learning lags
- Learned helplessness
- Aggressive behavior
- Lack of impulse control
- Promiscuous behavior

The infant who does not get her needs met becomes the child, then the adolescent, and, finally, the adult who carries these negative behaviors into her job, marriage, and friendships.

About the Disturbance (Diagnosis)

Physicians and therapists closely rely on the Diagnostic and Statistical Manual, Fourth Edition (DSM-IV), which is a compilation of conditions and their symptoms that details particular behaviors for the purpose of arriving at a diagnosis for any individual. The treatment that is implemented depends upon the primary diagnosis.

The vast range of underlying feelings and at-risk behaviors we have been discussing throughout this book converge into a single specialty area of understanding: diagnosing and treating kids with attachment disturbances.

This specialty is detailed in the DSM-IV and has become known as "Reactive Attachment Disorder" (RAD).[1]

It is necessary to point out that behaviors have been developed through one's personal history based on organicity, familial, and psychosocial, etc., factors. These behaviors have, in a sense, been chosen by the individual as a way to adapt to his surroundings in order to attempt to get his needs met – whether or not the chosen behaviors can be viewed as "normal" or "abnormal."

One of the concepts of neuro-linguistic programming (NLP) is, "Behind every behavior there exists a positive intention."[2] A child, based on – perhaps – painful early childhood illness, impoverished surroundings, poor modeling, neglect, abuse, etc., may have developed maladaptive behaviors. However, we *must* concentrate on the fact that, even when a youngster has developed a behavior that yields negative, harmful results, we still know that her intention is positive.

It is our role as clinicians and parents to specifically ascertain what the child's underlying needs and feelings are that are masked by maladaptive behaviors and the entire complex defense structure. The hope is to extinguish the defeating, distancing behaviors and help him replace them with more positive ones by addressing his real needs and true feelings.

Youngsters with RAD typically enter our program with severe disturbances in their behavior. Because their attachment cycles have been disrupted at such early ages, rendering them void of – or, at least, *lacking* in – the appropriate and necessary needs-fulfillment from their caregivers, they have developed maladaptive behaviors as a means of survival. These amazing children have discovered – probably through trial and error – an incredibly creative range of ways to fulfill their needs. They are characteristically bright and extraordinarily determined to become free from the Love Disorder and connect to adult caregivers to get what they really need.

    The uniqueness of any individual's behavior can tend to overlap into other DSM-IV diagnostic categories. Any individual's system of defense that has been activated by the pain of attachment disturbance can show symptoms of other specific diagnoses. Therefore, we see RAD as an umbrella diagnosis that can be the underlying origin of many other "more popular" diagnoses, such as Post Traumatic Stress Disorder, Attention Deficit Disorder, Attention Deficit with Hyperactivity Disorder, Conduct Disorder, Major Depression, Oppositional Defiant Disorder, and Multiple Personality Disorder. What are clinically known as Axis II diagnoses of Narcissistic, Dependent, Antisocial, and other personality disorders may also have underlying diagnoses of RAD. This is not to say that these diagnoses always have RAD as their origin, but the more popular diagnoses are often complicated and exacerbated by RAD's dynamics. DAT holds that healthy attachments provide a healthy basis for children to be better equipped to handle life's difficulties.

    The converse is also true. The more breaks in attachments for a child, the more vulnerable she is to life's pain – and therefore, the more likely she will be to create additional defenses to cope with that pain. Obviously, if a house is not built on a solid foundation, cracks in the structure are much more likely to occur than if the foundation were sound to begin with. So it is with Reactive Attachment Disorder – if an infant's attachment process is disturbed and the child has not been able to bond with her caregiver, she will lack the ego strength and the solid sense of self that is needed to cope in healthy and productive ways. This lack eventually results in her developing and exhibiting the maladaptive behaviors associated with these secondary diagnoses.

Research is providing us with some clear deliniations of the grouping of attachment symptoms. There seem to be definite, observable clusters of behavior that allow for attachment (and attachment disruptions) to be understood in terms of "types." These are discussed in the following chapter.

Chapter 13

Variations on a Theme

Secure Attachment

A child who is securely attached:

1. is able to use her mother as a secure base from which to explore her world.
2. expects his mother to respond to his signals.
3. cuddles into her mother and responds positively to behaviors such as smiling, laughing, hugging, and bouncing when being held.
4. experiences his contact with his mother as comforting and satisfying.
5. can accept it when her contact with her mother or other caregivers ceases.
6. is primarily cooperative and obedient and rarely angry.
7. develops "object permanence." At around the age of 1 year, he begins to know that when an object (caregiver) is not within sight, it does not cease to exist.
8. is able to express her needs in direct and appropriate manners and is persistent about getting those needs met.
9. is able to seek contact and be comforted when upset or frightened.
10. has tolerance for frustration and begins to develop problem-solving skills.

Yet, even for securely attached children, difficulties occur. This was true in Ricky's case. To understand his problems and make certain assessments about him, we were able to discern if and to what extent his problems were related to attachment disruptions.

Ricky

At 15, Ricky had what appeared to be, on the surface, a great life. School was okay, he had a solid family, he was a fairly good athlete, he had friends, and the future looked bright.

One morning I got a call, first thing, from Ricky's dad, Bob. Bob had heard about my work from one of his co-workers. I had spent some time working with this other man's son, who had been in trouble.

Bob got right to the issue: "I have a 15-year old son. Actually, I have three sons. But it's Ricky I'm calling about. He got arrested last night. The police called me at 2 a.m. Ricky and some – I don't know what you'd call them – "friends" – got caught down at the mall spray-painting buildings."

Bob was angry, disappointed, and at a loss. "I don't know what's wrong with the kid. Martin never had any problems. He's got everything he needs – "

During the next half-hour, I interviewed Bob and compiled a brief history of the family and Ricky. Bob was a lawyer for a high-powered firm. His wife, Cindy, had worked as an accountant. She had quit her job five years previously to spend more time at home with their 8-year-old son, Robert, Jr. Cindy volunteered about 20 hours a week at the hospital and the boys' schools.

Of their three boys, Martin, 19, was on an academic scholarship at Stanford. He was also an outstanding athlete and was expected to play baseball. From Bob's account, Martin would be pitching in the majors some day. Robert, Jr. was also "gifted." He was in a Gifted and Talented program at school, was quite precocious, and musically talented. He played the piano. That left Ricky.

Ricky was an "average" kid leading an "average" life. When I asked if there had been any major disruptions in their lives the past few years, Bob couldn't identify anything significant. He and Cindy had had some marital difficulties "mid-life," he explained, but nothing major. They had attended counseling and were "on top of the problem."

When Ricky had started ninth grade, however, he had had some difficulty. Always a B/C student, he suddenly started failing his classes. One of his counselors thought that Ricky might have attention problems and suggested that he get tested. Bob had taken him to a psychiatrist, who tested him and diagnosed him as having Attention Deficit Disorder, without hyperactivity (ADD). He prescribed Ritalin®, 50 mg. a day, and, during the next six months, Ricky seemed to improve.

"He was doing fine," Bob said. "Then, this."

I asked Bob if he thought Ricky was using.

"Using? I'm not sure I know what you mean."

I explained. "Is he smoking pot? Drinking?"

Bob's voice dropped. He seemed somewhat offended at the suggestion, then dismayed. "Of course not. I mean, there's no way. His brother never had any problems. Martin was a straight-A student. Ricky adores his brother. Besides this ADD thing, he's fine. Doesn't work as hard – "

"Have you noticed any changes in Ricky's behavior?" I listed the standard "warning" signs for drug use: change in appearance, appetite, erratic sleeping patterns, different peer group.

"Well, yes, we've seen all those things. I just thought it was the ADD."

I set up a time the following week to meet with the family.

Ricky was evaluated by one of our therapists who specializes in the treatment of chemical dependency. Ricky admitted that he had been drinking since he was 14 and recently had begun using marijuana once or twice a week with friends. He said he liked to drink beer and "smoke weed" to be able to talk more easily to people and because it helped him relax – especially when his parents weren't getting along. "I just want outta there when they're fighting," he said. He also said he felt like the dumb one in the family and that his parents loved his brothers more than him because they were so much smarter.

Because Ricky had been diagnosed with ADD – as are many attachment-disordered children – and because his mother had been ill for a month when Ricky was about 6 months old, his parents thought that, perhaps, Ricky had an attachment disorder.

What we found, however, was that Ricky's first two years, except for the month of his mother's illness, had been quite normal. His childhood behavior also sounded pretty normal even with the minor academic difficulties they reported. Moreover, he seemed to have a well-developed conscience, good internalized values, and showed a concern for others.

What *did* seem to be the problem was that Ricky was very angry about "feeling like the dumb kid in the family" and at his parents for their incessant fighting and coldness toward each other.

When we spoke with Ricky's mom, she confirmed that she and her husband had begun having marital difficulties shortly after Ricky's birth and that she, indeed, had been hospitalized for about a month with a severe viral infection when Ricky was about 6 months old. When she had come home from the hospital, it had seemed to take baby Ricky time to adjust to her again. But he soon was back to his normal, spunky self. She reported that he had been a happy baby and easy to care for. She also admitted that they had not planned on having another child when she became pregnant with Ricky – and if they did, they had wanted a girl. However, they had adjusted and felt they loved Ricky very much.

Our conclusion was that, although there were some disruptions in Ricky's attachment process, he lacked the symptoms associated with attachment disorder and had a secure attachment with his parents.

However, in addition to ADD, we believed that Ricky's use of drugs and alcohol were attempts at "self-medicating" the pain he felt about his parents' fighting and feeling like the dumb kid in the family. Because of all of these factors, we diagnosed him as having an Adjustment Reaction, as well as alcohol and cannabis abuse.

Ricky's core was intact, although it was shrouded with anger. His sense of self was somewhat poor – he perceived himself as "at the bottom of the totem pole" in his achievement-oriented, perfectionist family, where problems were not discussed but, instead, were "swept under the rug." Ricky, too, learned to deny problems and presented himself as an average, easy-going kid. He reacted to his anger and his perception of self by trying to escape through drug and alcohol use. Then, with pressure building to succeed academically – and with his parents' marital difficulties mounting – something had to give, and it did.

Please see the diagram of Ricky's defense structure in Figure 25.

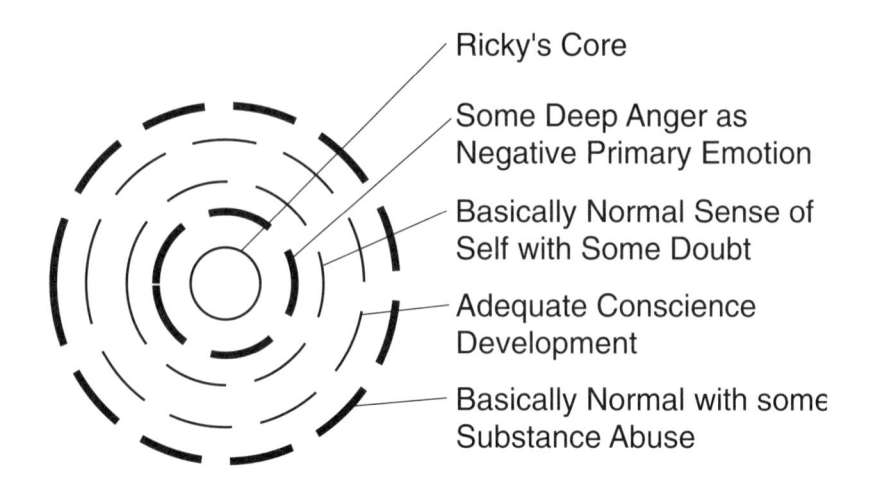

- Ricky's Core
- Some Deep Anger as Negative Primary Emotion
- Basically Normal Sense of Self with Some Doubt
- Adequate Conscience Development
- Basically Normal with some Substance Abuse

Figure 25

Ricky's Treatment

Ricky's treatment centered around his substance abuse. The addition of the family component provided the necessary forum for the family secrets and deep feelings all to surface. Bob and Cindy both had a little trouble hearing Ricky's feelings at first, but both were also open enough to appreciate what Ricky had been experiencing. The defeating family dynamics were successfully addressed and they have significantly improved their relationship.

Attachment Disorders

Although there are three main categories of attachment disorders, there are several characteristics that are common to each. These symptoms present in ways that are consistent with the layers of the defense structure discussed earlier. For diagnostic purposes, the DSM-IV can only deal with the observable and measurable outer layer of presenting symptoms. In other words, the true, underlying cause of the child's behavior may be masked by other, more obvious symptoms.

Attachment-disordered children are driven to be in control at all times. They engage in power struggles over the most trivial situations. For example, we were recently working with an 11-year-old in his home. He constantly wanted one of us to watch him play with his toys, but he could not tolerate our actually playing with his toys with him. He needed to control that distance precisely.

Attachment-disordered children also typically present themselves as having oral issues – the most common being hoarding and gorging on food. This can spin off into eating disorders, addiction to sweets, incessant chattering, speech delays, and incredibly articulate verbal arguing. These types of oral problems indicate attachment disruption that occurred both specifically around food deprivation itself but also generally about not getting needs met during that first year of life.

Disruptions during the second year of life also manifest later and present as anal issues. It is very common for attachment-disordered children to have bed-wetting and feces-smearing as symptomological behavior as late as ages 8, 9, and even into the teen years. The generalized behaviors from anal issues look like lack of impulse control ("I must have what I want, when I want it"). Further, the child can present as excessively stubborn, inflexible in thinking and acting, and rigidly perfectionistic.

Another typical behavior common to attachment disorders generally is "crazy lying" (lying when the truth would make more sense). This indicates the incredible strength of the child's refusal to become vulnerable to the adult even in trivial matters. This defense is very commonly used and is very difficult to deal with because the child is basically stating that he will not play by any reasonable rules. We have witnessed an adult reminding her 11-year-old son that he was not to eat the cookie he had in his mouth before dinner. The child, between mouthfuls, blurted out, "I'm not."

The inability to give or receive good eye contact, under-developed conscience, and poor cause-and-effect thinking are more examples of generic traits common to attachment-disordered children. Having discussed these throughout this section, we can now address the specific types of attachment disorder.

Anxious Attachment

As an infant, a baby who has formed what we call "anxious attachment" does have an attachment with her mother. She demonstrates the characteristics of a secure attachment to some extent (i.e., she looks to her mother for comfort in times of distress, etc.). But there exists an overriding, chronic level of anxiety in the relationship. Both the mother and the baby feel the insecurity in self and each other. Consequently, she acts generally upset and cries and gets angry easily and frequently. Moreover, she is very restricted in her willingness to explore her world and has difficulty tolerating even short-term separations from her mother.

As she grows older, she is likely to have poor peer relations and possibly school phobias. The latency-aged child (6 to 11 years old) is also very capable of occasional regressive behavior, such as thumb-sucking, bed-wetting, baby talk, senseless chatter, etc.

The anxiously attached child has a strong need to please his caregivers. He will literally give them the shirt off his back. This child is very likely to give away expensive toys or clothing (to please friends). Yet, typically, he will only allow himself to be cuddled, even when distressed, on his terms. When a parent initiates contact, he may superficially comply with a stiff hug, avoid eye contact, or squirm and push away – or even invent a physical ailment that would prohibit contact. This bind of craving closeness with caregivers yet fearing the vulnerability and, subsequently, pushing parents away keeps him full of the anxiety that he shows the world.

What is going on for the anxiously attached child is that she has taken a life stance that says, "The world is bigger, stronger, and more frightening than I can handle, so I will be constantly on the lookout (hypervigilant) for anything that can harm me. And, I better be at my best (never owning a mistake) to keep my only chance of survival intact (the umbilical cord with caregivers, especially Mom)." As a result, she seldom gets her needs met. This means that she is in a high state of arousal – remember the attachment cycle?

The tension that accompanies the need continues to be present in his body so that he cannot relax. This is why diagnoses such as ADD and ADHD show up so often. This is not a mis-diagnosis but, instead, a secondary cluster of symptoms that result from the more basic and pervasive diagnosis of RAD.

It is no wonder that the anxious child engages the world with superficial charm, compliance, crazy lying and excessive energy. She is attempting to not offend or alienate caregivers while, at the same time, needing to manage her world. Her logic seems to be, "I'm going to do things in such a way (perfectly *or* without responsibility or conscience) that no one can find fault with me. By being this way, I can control my universe." When this logic breaks down, the anxious child is very capable of any response, from sulking to full-blown tantrums. However, the truth is that, no matter what the response, she will rarely feel her body relax with the warm feeling of being loved, cared for, and nurtured.

We can better understand the dynamics of anxious attachment by taking a look Michelle's case. As an older teenager, Michelle's history and presenting problems indicated that she, in fact, was clearly attached to her parents, even though the relationship was riddled with anxiety that she absorbed and then eventually acted out.

Michelle

Michelle, at 17, was one of those teenagers who had managed to "slip through the cracks." She was attractive – blond hair, blue eyes, nice smile. She wore a bit too much make-up and was very self-conscious about her clothes. Her nails were perfectly manicured, candy-striped, and she had a small tattoo of a rose just above her ankle that was visible when she wore shorts.

Michelle was an only child. Her parents had divorced when she was 13, and she lived with her father. A week before she came to see me, she had overdosed on diet pills and alcohol.

When I met with her and her father, she sat passively and simply nodded her head "yes" or "no," depending on what she thought I wanted the answer to be. If I pressed her for an answer, her father intervened and answered for her. I finally asked him to leave and give us some time alone.

Michelle nervously clicked her nails on the top of my desk and stared down in her lap. I mentioned how interesting the candy stripes were. "How long does it take to do that?" I asked.

She shrugged. "Not long." She held out her hand, admiring her work, then added, "I want to be a beautician."

"I bet you'd be a good one," I offered. She looked away and seemed very uncomfortable. "How's school?"

"Okay, I guess."

" What's going on at home?"

"Nothing," she answered quickly.

"You getting along okay with your dad?"

She nodded and picked a piece of lint off her sweater.

"Your dad's worried about you. So's your mom." She raised her eyebrows, shrugged again.

"Should they be?"

"I guess," she finally said, as she started to squirm.

I smiled and waited. "Why?"

Her face suddenly changed and she started crying. Embarrassed, she put her hands up to cover her face. "Can I please leave?"

"Sure, if you promise to come back."

Michelle, stood, walked to the door, opened it, then turned suddenly. "My dad's out there. I don't want him to see me," she pleaded, shaking her hands.

"Uh, okay. I'll leave," I said, handing her a tissue. "You stay here. I'll be back in a few minutes."

After talking with Michelle's dad, he explained that he and his ex-wife had married young. They had felt overwhelmed and frightened by the arrival of baby Michelle. She had not been an easy baby; she was colicky until they discovered that she was allergic to cow's milk and found a special formula.

Although Mom had worried and doted over Michelle during her early years, she was not – according to Dad – a particularly warm or affectionate person. Dad described himself as loving his little daughter, but when she was a baby, he did little of the caretaking. Now that she was showing signs of womanhood, he was worried about being too close to her. He didn't want his affection to be misinterpreted. (Dad was protecting Michelle from his own sexual feelings.)

Michelle had always been shy and timid and somewhat slow developmentally. It had only been in the past few years that she had become more defiant: getting a tattoo, doing wild things to her hair, drinking, and taking drugs. For the most part, she had been quiet, self-effacing, and was someone people didn't really notice – which she used as part of her defense to control distance.

Even from the brief piece of Michelle's developmental history presented here, it is not difficult to understand why she had become an anxiously attached child. Infants who experience consistent pain or discomfort that is not relieved by the parents don't understand why their needs are not being met. They only know that no one is taking away their pain. In addition, if her mom worried and doted over her during her early years but was not a warm person,

Michelle undoubtedly would have sensed her mother's worries and fears and would have taken them on – but would not have felt really secure or loved. And later, with Mom pulling back from Michelle's care, Michelle could certainly have experienced that as her mom saying, "Dad, you take her, I have had enough!"

    As an anxiously attached child, Michelle steadily grew farther away from the shrinking safety zone of secure attachment toward more consistent "acting in" behavior. As a child, she expressed her anxiety by clinging passively, withdrawing, and obsessing about not being good enough. As a teenager, when it was no longer cool or socially acceptable to be too dependent, she covered her fears with more opposition and defiance. Her most serious cry for help, however, was her suicide attempt.

    Kids who "act in" often get overlooked or fall through the cracks because they are less openly destructive and rebellious. Therefore, they appear to be doing fine. After all, they are mostly compliant, not disruptive, overachievers. But there comes a point at which the anxious child begins to realize that the failure to get her needs met is not okay, and it can no longer be tolerated.

    In fact, Michelle had been deprived of the love and protection she deserved from her parents. She had reached this point, but because of her poor sense of self, she knew no other way to solve her problem – hence, the suicide attempt. This reaction came directly and predictably from her defense structure. See Figure 26:

- Michelle's Core
- Intense Fear as Negative Primary Emotion
- Very Weak Sense of Self
- Good but Rigid Conscience Development
- Moderately Difficult Presenting Problems

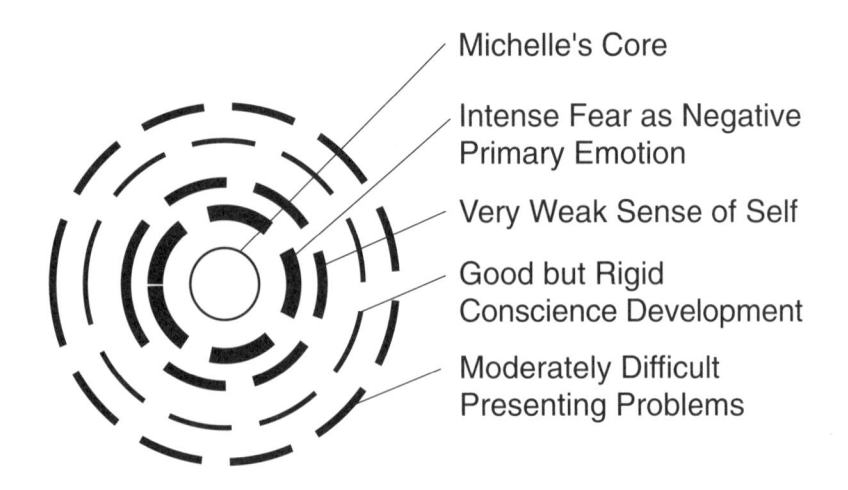

Figure 26

Working from the outside toward the core, we can see that Michelle's behavior, at least until the suicide attempt, had not been much of a problem. This is why she had been overlooked. She had never been quite "bad" enough to get her parents' or teachers' attention for professional help. However, her presenting problems began to escalate. Her acting-in behavior did not get her needs met, and she became more hostile and desperate as she reached that point of realization.

She certainly had good conscience development – perhaps *too* good. Michelle knew right from wrong but tended to exaggerate the wrong by constantly being self-effacing. Because of her poor sense of self, she was overly critical of her own performance and personhood. Her anxiety had led her into the stance that the world was too strong and threatening for her to cope with.

Further, any conflict with the world was her fault, in her opinion. This overactive, overscrupulous super-ego went hand in hand with the underdeveloped ego or self-concept. That lack of balance then kept her at the mercy of the world (caregivers) because she did not have the strength to express or accomplish getting her own needs met.

Michelle's primary negative emotion was fear – fear that no one was emotionally available for her – and even fear for her life when the pain (and the world) got to be too much for her. The infant Michelle believed that she could die from the pain and that there was no one who could protect her from it. This intense fear kept her from being in her real self (core) because she always had to be on guard (defensive) against it. And as long as she had to live in this defensive pattern, she continued to be deprived of developing her sense of self and saw herself as the problem. She was "stuck" in that cycle.

Michelle's Treatment

Before we could treat Michelle's attachment problems, we needed to stabilize her, assess her "at-risk" potential of another suicide attempt, and determine whether she could be treated as an out-patient. After she was fully evaluated, it was decided that Michelle could remain at home with her father and stepmother if she agreed to certain conditions:

1. that she would be in the house at all times and in someone else's company – not alone.
2. that she would be dressed in pajamas and slippers at all times unless she had to go to therapy appointments.

3. that she not use any drugs or alcohol during this period.
4. that she agree not to hurt herself or attempt suicide.
5. that if she felt like being self-destructive, she speak with her father, stepmother, or call us.

The point was to keep her safe, close, and, at the same time, to reestablish meeting her need to feel taken care of, protected, and loved. Her father and stepmother were instructed to spend generous amounts of time with her sharing various activities, such as playing cards, talking, reading together, etc.

Meanwhile, Michelle came to out-patient therapy three times a week. She talked about feeling lonely and stupid. She was able to recall several painful interactions with her mother, each that had the theme of Mom's impatience with her. Until then, Michelle had accepted her mom's blame as the truth.

We contacted Michelle's mother, who reluctantly agreed to become involved. Her message to us was, "She was always a good kid until Jerry and I split up. Then she blamed me. I mean, she was whiny and would always follow me around asking lots of dumb questions. But she was a very good child when she was little. Once she got older, however, she was often sullen and withdrawn. Occasionally, she'd explode over some dumb little thing. I didn't really know what to do for her, so Jerry took her. I see her every other weekend though. Also, she doesn't like my new boyfriend."

We worked with Michelle's mother to see if she would be able/willing to become more available to her daughter. We also asked if she would be willing to participate in Michelle's holdings. She balked at first, because

Jerry and his wife would be there. But then, she agreed. "I really love her, you know."

("Holding" is a therapeutic technique that involves literally holding the child comfortably. This is done by a team of two to four therapists for the purpose of keeping her safe and protected while she is encouraged to "re-visit" her early life trauma. Key to the process is her cathartic release of deep-seated emotions and traumatic memories that block her from forming loving, trusting relationships. During the process, she is not alone in her experience, as she was in the past. Instead, the therapists stay with her, validate her feelings, encourage her, show her that she can experience feelings, heightened arousal, and connection – and live through it. As the arousal state diminishes, the therapists or parents continue to meet her needs for touch, movement, and even food through cuddling, rocking, and feeding her, thereby building trust and relationship. This response by the therapists/parents provides what is known as the "emotional corrective experience.")

Michelle did well during her two-week pajama party. She was able to meet all of her contracts with us and reported that, indeed, she felt more taken care of, protected, and loved. This set the stage for the series of holdings we had planned with our team, her father and stepmother, and her mother.

During her holdings, Michelle was able to:
1. identify and express her deep primary negative feelings.
2. recognize when and how she defended against the pain of her early life.
3. begin to "let herself off the hook" by recognizing the truth about her pain.
4. see herself as good and worthy.

    5. begin to acquire the necessary skills to engage the world, her mother, and herself in more open, honest, and effective ways.

As so often happens during the use of our DAT family systems approach, we needed to quickly shift our efforts to the parents. Michelle was getting better – no one questioned that. But in order to receive her daughter in a new, productive manner, Michelle's mother needed to do her own work focused on her issues of her relationship with her own mother. She was able to do enough healing during our holdings to have the courage to continue to work in the new, genuine ways that we were promoting. She committed to continuing her own therapy and to learning how to be available to Michelle. She proved to be a hard worker at going after what she had always wanted but never knew how to get – a close relationship with her daughter.

With this response from her mom, Michelle blossomed during the intensive. She actually looked fuller and more womanly when we finished. She was not done with her work – she still needed practice developing her insights and skills. She also needed affirmation of herself and her femininity. This was an ongoing process for her to "practice" with both her father and her mother. But they were all finally in a new position: to be able to both give and receive. Dad was able to accept her as a pretty young woman without needing to hold back to protect his feelings; Mom was able to initiate mother-daughter activities that they both enjoyed. At last report, they felt very positive their new relationships, and Michelle had begun dating a young man who had actually gained Mom's approval.

Avoidant Attachment

Because of early life trauma, the avoidantly attached child has concluded that adults – especially the ones who are supposed to care for them, protect them, and love them – cannot be trusted and are to be avoided at all costs. He has learned to survive by ignoring his own emotions and becoming what we call *self-parenting*.

We have come to realize that this dynamic is a response by the child to a hostile world characterized by pain and fear, betrayal, rejection, abandonment, and/or neglect. If the baby is separated from Mom, she will be rejecting of Mom upon her return.

This child learns the reversed behavior patterns of not showing need or vulnerability at an early age. When the toddler is picked up to play, or if a parent tries to comfort him, he will push away and basically try to take care of the problem himself. As he grows older, he is likely to become aggressive and defiant toward authority. This, of course, will provoke the ire of teachers and make it difficult for him to fit into any peer group other than with rebels like himself. Even adolescence and adulthood are marked by social isolation. If there are any peer or love relationships, they are likely to be marked by jealousy and possessiveness because the avoidantly attached person also must control his universe.

The lack of interaction with adult caregivers also prevents the child from having anyone to help her separate normally and naturally from in the process of individuation. *The lack of this vital interaction is a prime reason for an underdeveloped conscience and unclear, undefined sense of self.* This handicap limits the sense of empathy this individual has for the pain or difficulties of others. Predictably, she cannot begin to understand others' pain when she cannot feel her own.

However, the avoidantly attached child can't sustain this "shut-down" stance for long. Aggressive outbursts toward his family and cruelty to animals is often a selected outlet. He is also often destructive but in passive-aggressive ways. He either "accidentally" destroys things to hurt people or does it when no one is looking – all without responsibility or conscience.

It is easy to understand that the avoidantly attached child may carry other labels (diagnoses), such as Conduct Disorder, Character Disorder, Antisocial Personality Disorder, and Paranoid Personality Disorder. His isolation and self-parenting style is seen as antisocial and paranoid. His distrust and hostility manifest as Conduct Disorder, and his cruelty and lack of conscience can be understood as character-disordered. Each of these diagnoses can be accurate, but, again, each is secondary to the primary problem of Reactive Attachment Disorder.

This was true of A.J. This boy was typical of the problem many Americans are experiencing with foreign adoptions. Certainly, avoidant attachment is not limited to this history. In fact, this Character Disorder, sociopathic personality, was the first type of attachment disorder to really be studied by Foster Cline and others. This is a very pervasive and difficult disorder to treat. It is the epitome of the Love Disorder because the child so blatantly refuses – or is unable – to accept or to give love.

A.J.

By the age of 10, A.J. had seen more of the dark side of life than most people ever do. He had been shuffled from foster home to foster home until he was finally adopted at age 5 by a young couple, John and Mary, who couldn't have children of their own. They had spent years and thousands of dollars with artificial methods. Although Mary had become pregnant several times, she had always miscarried.

John and Mary's story, while unique in its own ways, was also representative of a number of couples I had worked with who had also adopted children. John, 32, was a computer programmer, and Mary, 30, was an elementary school teacher. They had met in college, married soon after graduation, and, after landing jobs and buying a home, were ready to start a family.

"I wanted lots of kids," John had explained in one of our first sessions. Mary had smiled less enthusiastically, and had said, "I thought three kids would be just right. He wanted a baseball team."

After years of frustration, and with no guarantee that they would have their own children, they decided to adopt. They found an agency recommended by a friend, completed all the interviews, the voluminous paperwork, and waited.

Then one morning, they got the call that a 5-year-old boy was available – in Korea. "I remember I canceled all my appointments, called the school, and pulled Mary out of class. We had everything arranged, then we left that evening."

"It was September 21," Mary added. "I had just started the school year. It was tough to leave my kids, but we had discussed it in class. They were as excited as I was."

The next day, they met their son, A.J. "I'll never forget the first time I saw him," Mary said, as she squeezed John's hand. "His foster mom was holding him so he had his back toward us. He was wearing this cute blue jumper and these adorable sandals. Then she turned around and I saw his face." Mary smiled, held up a hand and her voice dropped to a hush. "I fell in love with him immediately. He was just how I pictured him."

"He had no problems coming to us," John had said. "I was surprised, actually. He walked right over. I held out my arms, and he let me pick him up." He paused for a moment. "There was one thing, though. He didn't smile. In fact, in the year we've had him, I don't think he's smiled more than once or twice." Mary nodded her head quietly in agreement.

Unfortunately, the "honeymoon" with A.J. had been short-lived. Almost immediately, they began to have problems. A.J. had horrible night terrors and woke up shrieking. "We brought his bed into our room," John had begun, "but now, none of us sleep."

A.J. also had a tough transition into school. Understandably, his English was limited, but he also was behind with his numbers and with gross and fine motor skills. He was tested and placed into special education.

"Almost immediately, the fights started," John began, grim-faced. "We hoped he was just adjusting, but it got worse. He bit one little girl clear down to the bone in her hand."

"That's when they asked us to pull him out," Mary added. "That's when I decided to take a year off from teaching and home-school A.J. He started having tantrums and throwing things. Then he bit me." Mary's frustration really came out when she confessed in a sheepish way that they had had A.J. in therapy almost entirely during the five years since his adoption. "We've seen four or five therapists and psychiatrists, and nothing seems to help. We've tried Ritalin®, Depakote®, and even lithium, but it only seems to drug him up and does nothing to change his behavior."

"The final straw," John said, shifting uncomfortably on the couch, "was when we found the cat."

"What happened?" I asked.

"He'd been stabbed in the side," John pointed to his ribs, "and one of his ears had been torn nearly off."

"Could it have been another cat or dog?"

John and Mary looked at each other, and almost simultaneously they shook their heads. "I found A.J. in the kitchen, crying, with a pair of scissors. There was a huge scratch across his arm and blood all over the kitchen floor."

"That's when we decided to call you," Mary said, looking up at me.

※   ※   ※

What had happened to the cute child John and Mary thought they'd be bringing home with them – the child who had opened his arms and gone immediately into their embrace at the airport? Why was he not bonding with them, and why was he hurting other children and animals? How could a child appear so cute and innocent and act so demonic?

Although very little information was available about his birth parents, we learned that he had been taken from his birth-mother at the age of 18 months because of abuse and neglect. He was unable to stay at various foster homes for unknown reasons, but by the age of 5, he had been in four foster homes.

Here was a child who had given up on trying to get the love and nurturing he needed because he knew that either he wouldn't get it or it would be ripped away from him. A.J. was a child who looked cute and knew how to turn on the charm (for short periods of time, at least) but who was enraged at being deprived of his primal needs. He displaced his anger at those who had abused and neglected him by killing animals and hurting his classmates. He might also injure animals or other children whom he perceived were getting what he failed to get.

One might think: "But he was getting nurtured now, and John and Mary were doing everything for this child."

That couldn't help until A.J. could repair the trust that was so badly damaged in his early years, when the attachment cycle was repeatedly disrupted.

A.J. was at high risk on the outer limits of the Shrinking Safety Zone. He was an avoidantly attached child. He didn't really allow closeness with his caretakers, expressed his rage by acting out with little or no remorse, and was indiscriminately affectionate with strangers. Another way of looking at him was through the layers of his defense structure.

His behavioral symptoms of severe aggression and cruelty toward people and animals were major barriers to his core; so was his lack of developed conscience, which allowed him to do hurtful deeds without remorse. His poor self-concept was also a difficult barrier to penetrate. His negative primal emotions were less of a barrier except when they produced the secondary symptoms – his behaviors. Using our diagram of the defense structure, A.J.'s looked like Figure 27.

A.J.'s Core

Moderate Negative Primary Emotions

Very Weak Sense of Self

Significant Lack of Conscience Development

Major Barrier of Presenting Problems

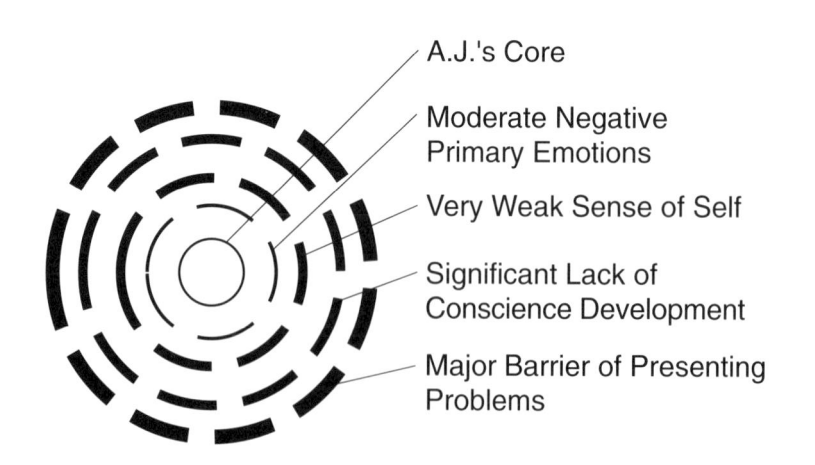

Figure 27

A.J.'s Treatment

To determine a course of treatment for A.J. and his family, many things needed to be assessed and considered. Several factors convinced us to follow the DAT 10-day intensive protocol:

1. A.J.'s early-life trauma, which caused severe breaks in his ability to attach to his caregivers;
2. The very tough defense structure he employed to insulate himself from further pain;
3. The critical nature of the presenting problems (i.e., killing animals, biting people).
4. The fact that all other therapeutic modalities had failed with him;
5. John and Mary's good mental health and strength were available to provide a secure safety zone; and
6. A.J. himself realized that his life was not working, and he was able to contract with us to do this intensive work.

Because John and Mary were at the end of their individual and collective ropes and felt that they had tried and failed at every possible intervention with their son, they were very open to establishing a new "bottom line" in the structure of their discipline.

In this case, the bottom line was drastic: A.J. was placed in one of our therapeutic foster homes during the intensive and afterward until his behavior showed us that he could trust and allow himself to be parented. This goal was measured by evidence of decreased aggression in cruelty to animals, no more biting, less fighting and arguing. He was also expected to demonstrate the ability to cooperate, follow rules, and be affectionate on parental terms. As his behavior improved, he was deemed able to handle living at home and began by having more frequent visits with John and Mary.

The therapeutic foster home served several purposes: it let A.J. know that there were consequences for his behavior; it gave his beleaguered parents a rest; and it provided an environment where parents already trained in the Partnership Model cared for him.

During the intensive, we worked with John, Mary, and A.J. all present. We also had the therapeutic foster parents participate in some sessions so that they could get to know A.J. and experience his issues first-hand. As we held him, we were also modeling for the parents how to set limits, what to reasonably expect behaviorally, and how to recreate the attachment cycle. The holdings also demonstrated the "how to" of the concept of bringing him in closer when he was struggling. During the 10 sessions, we also focused on and held both parents, which allowed them to experience the holding for themselves and provided them with the opportunity to do some purging of their own pain.

Most of the sessions, however, were geared toward helping them work with A.J. in a new and more effective manner. During some holdings, A.J. seemed happy and bright that he was releasing his "big feelings." Yet, at other times, he acted somewhat aloof and indifferent to the process, as if he were afraid that he had made himself too vulnerable. This repeated use of old defenses finally gave way to some incredible depth of expression of the pain and fear that he had experienced in his early life. Toward the end of the 10 sessions, he was finally able to reach for his mother and embrace her. As she held her son and assured him of her never-ending love for him, he was able to look into her eyes and say, "I love you, Mom."

By the end of the intensive, A.J. was a changed child. He smiled more and his face and body were definitely more relaxed. He was more cooperative and was genuinely affectionate with both parents.

His work in the therapeutic foster home went well. It was basically centered around building an honest and accurate sense of self by "practicing" accepting caring and worth from his foster parents. With follow-up outpatient therapy planned for, A.J. and his parents were reunited after about three months.

Ambivalent Attachment

The ambivalently attached child is a paradox on two legs. He can present himself as *either* anxiously attached *or* avoidantly attached, acting out the clusters of symptoms that indicate each of those disorders. But, actually, this apparent dichotomy of behavior is a response to its own unique cluster of symptoms. Ambivalent attachment is characterized by this "either-or," "all-or-nothing," and "black-or-white" thinking. "If I can't have it my way, I just won't do it." "If you love Jimmy, then you can't love me." "If I can't have three oranges, then I won't have any."

As infants, these children cry to be picked up, fuss while being held, then fuss even more when put down. They are rarely satisfied. If separated from Mom even for a short time, they may greet her enthusiastically – and then kick her in the shins. They tend to be clingy and compliant children one minute – and then rejecting and hostile to parents the next.

These kids are caught in the bind of desiring closeness from caregivers – but they are also terrified of the very same closeness they crave. As a result, they oscillate – back and forth and back and forth – and work hard to achieve closeness. However, when that becomes too scary, or they don't get what they want, *they work hard to gain distance by doing whatever is necessary, without regard to the well-being of self or others.* They are caught in this cycle and can't get out. This feeling of being trapped both *enrages* and *depresses* them, which is consistent with the paradox they live. They are angry they can't get what they want or need *and* feel helpless and hopeless (depressed) that they can't do anything about it.

As teens, they realize that it is socially unacceptable to act out their neediness *and* dangerous to act out their rage. So they shut down and control themselves. This strategy leaves them withdrawn, oblivious to their authentic feelings, and depressed until they can't hold it any longer. (I've heard teens admit they have no clue as to how they feel.) Then they repeat the cycle by exploding in rage or provoking someone to the point of flying off the handle at them. Or, since they can't stand being shut down, they relieve the inner tension by creating some stimulation through various degrees of high-risk activity. They may binge eat, shop lift, use drugs/alcohol, drive recklessly, engage in gun play, gesture suicide, or even self-mutilate.

Ambivalently attached teens become very skillful in developing a "push-pull" style of relating to people. When in their "anxious" phase, they tend to idealize the object (person) in the relationship. They can charm and manipulate to "entice" them into their schemes of getting what they want. And, when they are in their "avoidant" phase, they possess the venom necessary to push away even the most caring adult or loyal friend. This borderline personality style gives them exactly what they think they want – control. And, like the other types of attachment disorders, this cluster of symptoms becomes an integral part of the defense structure needed to protect the child from the Pain

Gap – the pain of being close to and trusting caregivers and then not getting needs met.

The ambivalent attachment is the "modern" adaptation in the RAD field. I believe it has surfaced complete with its own identity because what it really comes from is anxious attachment. But because it is not at all "cool" for a pre-teen or teen to look and act like they have anxiety, they over-compensate and do everything they can to look like they don't care, are indifferent, and without need. That explains the oscillating back and forth, in and out of closeness with adult caregivers. Meet Kerry, who was a very interesting example of ambivalent attachment.

Kerry

The first time I met Kerry, she appeared to be a typical 16-year-old. When she came to my office with her mother, I was immediately impressed with her interpersonal skills and her energy. Her mother, on the other hand, seemed exhausted and depressed. They were quite a contrast.

I have a small office, a desk, a couple of "pilot" seats, a dying fern, a couple of inspirational posters. Kerry made herself at home, plopping into a chair, spinning around, and taking in the surroundings. She came across as overly familiar, self-confident – even defiant – and could talk with authority about any topic, as I soon discovered. She had intense green eyes and looked me straight in the eye, as if she was waiting for me to challenge her. Her most striking feature was her close-cropped, fluorescent purple hair, which she had recently colored.

Her mother sat next to her, clutching her purse on her lap. She fidgeted and forced a smile when I tried to put her at ease. The dark circles under her eyes spoke volumes about the turmoil and tension the family had been struggling with.

From Mom's perspective, Kerry was out of control. She consistently broke curfew, was hanging out with the "wrong" people, and "doing I don't know what!" Kerry wouldn't listen to her or her husband (Kerry's step-father), was failing in school, and she "just didn't care."

While Kerry's mom voiced her list of complaints, Kerry rolled her eyes, smiled wryly, sat back, and put her feet up on the edge of my desk.

"Mom," she began in a tired voice, "it's no big deal. We just go down to the coffee house."

"That place isn't safe," her mother returned, facing me. "There are dealers down there…"

"Oh, please," Kerry interrupted, holding up a hand. "You don't know, so just shut up."

From there, the conversation deteriorated. The mother continued to announce her list of complaints, and Kerry listened only long enough to dispute each one. After about 15 minutes, Mom finally wore down. Kerry, sensing this, took the opportunity to pounce on her.

Her speech seemed to be one she had saved, her ace-in-the-hole attack for when she wanted to hurt her mother. She turned in her chair to face her mom, put her feet on the floor, sat forward, and jabbed a finger at her mother's face. Her mother, startled, flinched and sat back.

"Maybe if you'd been around at night instead of staying out with George, I would have felt like coming home. Maybe if you would have saved some of your precious time for me – "

"We were there, Kerry. For dinner – "

"Yeah, right. There's no fuckin' way I'm gonna' let George boss me around and tell me how I'm supposed to look to eat dinner." Kerry sat back and hugged herself tightly as she pulled her legs up and sat cross-legged.

"I don't know what you're talking about," her mother offered, almost in a whisper.

"Bullshit. I tried. I came to dinner, and George ordered me to change my pants. Fuck that."

"Watch your language."

"Oh, fuck you," Kerry whispered under her breath, but loud enough for her mom to hear.

"See?" her mother asked, staring at me, stone-faced. "See what I have to deal with?"

I asked Kerry to leave the room while I spoke with her mom. The dance Kerry and her mother were doing was now very obvious. Kerry had learned how to wear down her mother while her mother had become resigned – if not immune – to her daughter's abusive treatment. The more Kerry acted aggressively toward Mom, the more Mom wouldn't hear her daughter. The more she wouldn't hear, the "louder" (more aggressive) Kerry got.

I asked Marcy, Kerry's mom, about her pregnancy with Kerry and Kerry's first two years. Marcy recounted that she had been 19 when she became pregnant. Her new husband had not wanted to have a baby – he spent a great deal of time drinking and hanging out with his friends. In fact, he would often stay out all night.

Marcy admitted being depressed throughout her pregnancy but held the hope that the birth of the baby would improve matters. Kerry's birth was not unusual in any way, but Marcy's feelings of depression and of being alone to raise this child deepened with her husband's continued lack of interest in the baby. Often, he would come home drunk, and they would get into terrible fights. As the fights became more frequent and violent, Marcy decided to leave her husband and move in with her mother. Kerry was 2 years old.

During that time, Kerry became clingy to her mother and refused to leave her side. At other times, she was fussy and would not let anyone (including Marcy) comfort her. When her parents divorced, she showed no signs of missing her father. As Kerry got older, she sometimes became belligerent with her mother, her friends, and her teachers. At other times she was friendly, almost affectionate, and a model student. She had friendships at school, but her relationships seemed peppered with fights and were "on-again, off-again" at best. Her actions often seemed to say, "I need you *and* I won't let you take care of me."

Kerry's behavior in my office seemed consistent with the history that Marcy had given me. She acted like she wanted the closeness, wanted her mom around – but when Marcy and George were there (for dinner), Kerry found something wrong with it. She wouldn't accept her mother's caring.

Kerry acted like an ambivalently attached child. She showed that she wanted closeness, but when she actually got it, she rejected it. In traditional DSM-IV diagnostic terms, Kerry met the criteria for Oppositional Defiant Disorder with the strong beginnings of a Borderline Personality Disorder.

Kerry's Treatment

In order to treat Kerry, we had to first work with Marcy and George to help them heal and become strong enough to provide the necessary tough-yet-loving structure that Kerry needed so desperately. Kerry was calling out for someone to care enough to see through her disguise of not needing or wanting closeness and guidance. At the same time we were working with Marcy and George, we began to help Kerry with her assignment: to receive the care and direction her parents had for her.

This movement, of course, meant that many things had to shift for Kerry. She also had to be healed from her difficult early life; her tough defense structure had to be dealt with, and her core had to be reached to give her the hope necessary to continue with changing her life and her relationship with her parents.

George was very angry about all the abuse Kerry dished out to Marcy and because Kerry's acting out was often disruptive and divisive to their marriage. Marcy was often depressed – as she had been for so long during Kerry's early life. George and Marcy agreed to work with us in family therapy, and Marcy also agreed to individual treatment for her depression.

We set up a series of holdings for Kerry using Dynamic Attachment Therapy principles, while we modeled and engaged her with the Partnership Model of Discipline. She had no problem contracting with us to do this work – she admitted that she had "a good feeling" about us and that she was tired of the fighting. She wanted to feel better about herself and her parents.

Reaching Kerry's core in therapy was not as difficult as I had originally thought it would be. She showed remarkable trust and motivation to work with our direction in her holdings. Very quickly, she was able to revisit her early-life trauma and give us her primary accompanying feelings of rage, despair, and terror.

Working our way outwardly from there, we all came to realize how fragile her sense of self was. She had shown glimpses of wanting relationships and love, but actually *feeling* that need for others provoked too much anxiety in her and left her too vulnerable to pursue getting what she wanted and needed. Her sense of self just wasn't strong enough to deal with the threat of being hurt by others. Those feelings, in turn, caused her to defend strongly by provoking others – so they would not get too close to her. A diagram of Kerry's defense structure follows in Figure 28:

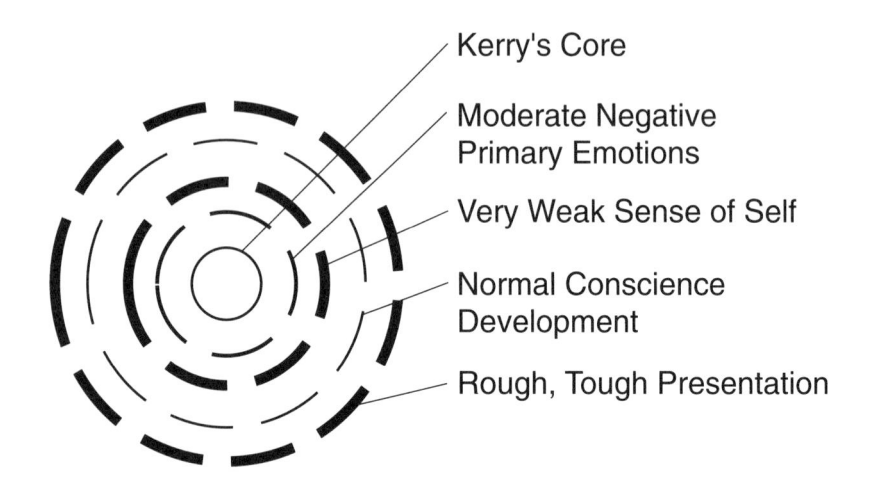

- Kerry's Core
- Moderate Negative Primary Emotions
- Very Weak Sense of Self
- Normal Conscience Development
- Rough, Tough Presentation

Figure 28

Although Kerry often acted to the contrary, as we gradually peeled away her defense structure, we were able to see a conscience that really was authentic. She honestly felt bad about the entire family mess and her abusive behavior. This dynamic of acting out abusively – seemingly with no remorse, when, in fact, she *did* feel awful about it – is very typical of the ambivalent attachment itself.

With therapy, Marcy healed enough that she had renewed vigor about setting fair-but-consistent limits with Kerry, and George supported her in doing so. If Kerry stayed out past her curfew, she did not go out that next week. Marcy began to reel Kerry in, spending lots of time with her. They made an agreement that, if Kerry couldn't control her screaming, swearing, and blaming, they would scream together for as long as it took for Kerry to feel better. Only then would they attempt to resolve the issue at hand.

School was left, in large part, to Kerry and her teachers. Marcy and George were able to back off the pressure they had been giving Kerry about school performance as they began to accept that failure would be *her* problem. They were finally able to give her the message, "Your school will offer ninth grade again next year, so if you need to fail, you will be taken care of." That was not to say that Marcy or even George weren't available to help with school work and ideas when Kerry asked.

Although she still had her moments of lying, swearing, and pushing people away, she got better at letting Marcy and George parent her and letting their love and guidance matter to her. She also was able to try harder at school and to treat her teachers with more respect and appreciation. Kerry has since graduated from high school and is attending community college, holding a job, and still living at home.

We believe that this turnaround for Kerry and her mom and stepfather could only happen as a result of each of them confronting their own pain and ineffective ways of coping with it.

For Kerry, it took courage and trust to enter into this intense work to address the pain her infant self had experienced (perhaps even in the womb) because her parents had been too preoccupied with their own depression and anger. As an infant, Kerry had felt unloved, a concept that she internalized. More specifically, she had most likely felt loved at the times when her mother had been willing and able to give love or needed love herself. But Kerry had not felt the love that would have come with consistently getting her basic needs met as a baby. No wonder she was ambivalent.

In our sessions, Kerry began to learn that it was safe to be vulnerable with people who loved her and that she could be herself and still be loved and cared for. She also gradually learned from her parents' words and actions that they offered her a "safety zone" from which she could live her life.

Section Five
Love is Lovelier the Second Time Around

Kids who can't love or be loved do, indeed, need a "second time around." The first time sure didn't work out for them or provide them with the tools and wherewithal for success in loving relationships. Most of these kids were abused, neglected, abandoned, or victims of illness, inadequate parenting, poor genetics, alienated families, multiple placements, and, perhaps, a "system" that didn't understand them and couldn't work with them. We need to change the system and the thinking of adult caregivers. We need to educate parents and professionals about the dynamics of attachment and what happens when attachment is disrupted. Then we can provide these adults with the tools that can promote optimal partnering and optimal results for their children. These children deserve a second chance. The love *can* be lovelier the second time around, but it must be done with a new paradigm and a new, enlightened set of principles and tools.

Chapter 14

Attachment Principles

The partnership model of discipline is composed of specific principles: the attitudes, intentions, and techniques that the adult partner needs to understand and implement in order to parent the attachment-disrupted child effectively. The intention of this model is to promote the child's ability to learn to sustain successful long-term interpersonal relationships. In order to achieve this, his defense structure must be penetrated so that a "heart-to-heart" connection can be made between him and the adult professional.

In the workshops and lectures we give around the country, we are invariably asked, "What should I do when…?" This is a great question – if we are to consider that each of the child's problem behaviors is separate from another and that there is no pattern or theme of consistency to them. If we answer that question outside of the context of the entire model, we are implying that this is the case. And that means we are solving one problem at a time. The ancient Chinese proverb applies here: Give a man a fish, and he will eat for a day; *teach* him how to fish, and he will eat for a lifetime. We teach a parenting model, based on attachment principles, that addresses the entire package as opposed to isolated behaviors. We offer a lifetime of healthy relationships – not just behavior management.

Create the Velvet Box

The velvet box is the context or the treatment milieu within which the child is placed. While it isn't a literal, physical box, it does define the acceptable limits and boundaries of her behavior. The outside walls of this imaginary box are *just* broader than her abilities. This extra room allows her to stretch, grow, and to make some fairly non-traumatic choices. These walls should be flexible – to expand and contract as her ability to handle life ebbs and flows and matures. Children, especially these difficult ones, want to be contained. They do not want to be "out of control." That is why they defend so strongly against their "killing feelings."

The box is a container. It keeps the child safe and under control – whether it is in his home life, the therapist's office, or the rules for being out in public. We "hold" (contain) him when he is in our presence, in our partnership, in our gaze, in our thoughts and energy – literally, for nurture or safety.

The meaning of the velvet is that all of this is done with a soft hand. This concept is borrowed from the Buddhist principle of "compassion with calm detachment." There is compassion and nurturing *for* the child, yet the calm detachment *from* her allows her to take on the responsibilities and the freedom to develop her sense of self. Further, calm detachment helps eliminate any confusion about whose job it is to function within the box. It also identifies who has had a problem with lying, the court, or the law that originally put her in this box. It clearly defines who is the child, who is the adult, and the roles of each.

The outside walls of the box and the quality of functioning within the box are constantly defined and reinforced by the continuous use of feedback from the adult partner. This feedback comes in the form of "high confrontation/high support." It looks much like the childhood game "You're getting warm, warmer – oh, you're hot now;" or, "You're getting cold, colder" – until "You're ice cold."

Similarly, "Jimmy, I really like how you handled that upset," or, "Great job of sharing your bicycle," or, "I really don't like the way you are acting at the dinner table right now. I care about you and you are entitled to your feelings, *and* you are accountable for your behavior." Using the principle of high confrontation and high support means that, although we may not accept the behavior, we support the fact that kids have these valid feelings.

The box must be constructed prior to and independently of meeting any children. The materials used are derived from the prerequisites we mentioned earlier. Your insight into your own strengths and weaknesses, your understanding of partnering with children, and your knowledge of the attachment disorder itself will be the materials from which you build the box for each child. Once you add the velvet touch, you are prepared for children to begin their passage through your professional, supportive territory. You are ready to practice the attachment principles and use the tools that implement them.

Work in Partnership

Know that every interaction, every intervention, every contact with the child occurs within the definition of your unique relationship with him. Keep the two goals of partnership constantly in mind. It's not a partnership of equal say – but one of equal commitment to see the child through his passage. As a partner, you are not the authoritarian "boss" who is always right, always healthy, or always sees him as wrong, corrupt, dangerous, sick, incompetent, or stupid.

Instead, you:
1. see the child as good (with a core worthy of redemption).
2. balance empathy and accountability. This is our way of understanding and behaving in ways that accept the child unconditionally while holding her accountable for her behavior. "I can understand that you were mad at your sister (and I accept you and will continue to care for you) – but it's not okay for you to act that way."
3. promote cooperation, not merely compliance. Of course, there is a time when the adult wants and must insist on immediate compliance (such as insisting that the child take your hand when you cross a busy street together). I suppose that an adult could force a child into compliance about cleaning his room, for example – but at what price? This type of message – that the adult is bigger and stronger than he is and can, therefore, do whatever she wants to do to him – is coercive and often reflects his earlier life trauma. He might comply, but someone will usually pay for it through some aggressive or passive-aggressive response from him. Promoting cooperation gives him room to make choices, learn from consequences, and further trust his partner – all while gaining a greater sense of self. It increases the "elasticity" of the partnership.
4. insist on the reciprocal response. When we do this, we give the message that it is not okay for the child to ignore you, avoid you, or distance from you. In other words, your response should convey, "I want a relationship with you, and your response is important to me." Healthy interpersonal relationships involve a willingness to give to and receive from each other. The ability to

reciprocate also indicates a degree of openness toward being loved and loving in return.

5. help define the question, "Whose problem is it?" This makes it very clear whose responsibility it is to deal with the problem. If, indeed, it is *her* problem, we have room to practice partnering by giving compassion, creating gifts, and acting as a consultant to her: "Good luck on this. If you need any ideas, let me know, because I am available and I care how you do with this problem."

6. negotiate, make deals, and get contracts (complete with consequences). Distinguish between what's "negotiable" and what's "non-negotiable." "You and me – we agree." (Although this may not sound easy to do, skillful partners have high success rates with their young clients. If agreement can't be reached, then we do it "the hard way" – which is the adult's best guess as to what is best for the child). This approach promotes partnership, trust, and responsibility. It puts the reciprocal response into practice: "You paint my fence, and I will give you an agreed-upon amount of money." We always look for a "shake-hands deal." It also recreates the attachment cycle by stating needs and the conditions of getting them met in clear, accurate statements.

Recreate the Attachment Cycle Whenever Possible

Attachment-disordered children are needy – often very needy. In addition, once a child is placed in the adult partner's care (the velvet box), needs are automatically created around freedoms of speech, movement, and participation in activities. Our job as adult partners is to recreate the successful completion of the attachment cycle. To refresh your memory, see Figure 29:

The Attachment Cycle

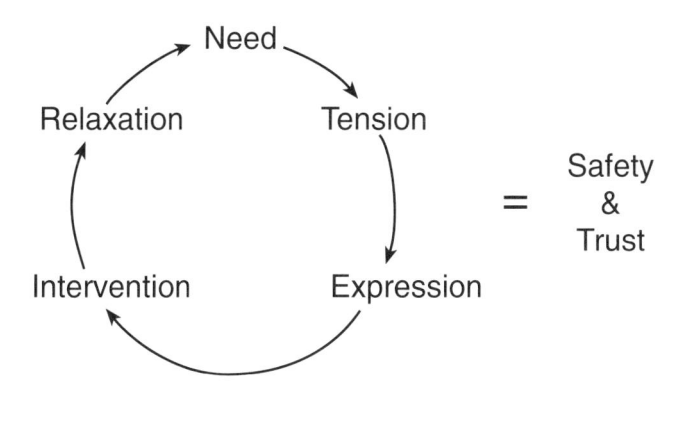

```
         Need
Relaxation   Tension
                       Safety
              =         &
                       Trust
Intervention   Expression
```

Figure 29

    To facilitate the completion of the cycle, we must 1) realize that the child is needy, 2) recognize her expressions of trying to get her needs met, and 3) provide the most effective intervention possible to meet those needs. This helps the child relax, complete the cycle, and increase her feelings of safety about and trust toward her partner. This provides what is traditionally referred to as an "emotionally corrective experience."

    The whole idea behind recreating the attachment cycle is to correct the emotional experience(s) that ended in trauma in the child's early life. However, because he is with a practiced adult partner, when he expresses a need *this* time, that need is met. He is not ignored, abused, criticized or abandoned. He gets to *experience** being cared for – and the successful completion of the cycle. In DAT, we believe that, for the disorder to be reversed, the child must quantitatively *experience** more cycle successes than he experienced* cycle disruptions earlier in life.

*Please note: The reason for the emphasis on "experience" is to put forth the rationale that traditional sit-up-and-talk therapies are not effective with attachment-disordered children. DAT is based on the premise that the nature of the therapy has to be the same as the nature of the trauma – experiential – not to re-traumatize but to re-visit the trauma through an emotionally corrective experience. Therefore, we always look for new shared experiences that can enhance the quality of the bond between adult and child partners.

The following are the tools the adult must use to facilitate the successful completion of the attachment cycle with the child:

1. Explore and then connect to her motivation and goals for this passage with you.
2. Provide the basics:
    a. Give and insist on good eye-contact.
    b. Give warm, loving touch.
    c. Provide movement, such as rocking and bouncing.
    d. Demonstrate affection regardless of response.
3. Be available to hear/negotiate/fulfill his needs as much as possible.
4. Help the child express her needs appropriately and in words.
5. Give immediate responses to appropriate requests. (Sometimes that response is, "I need to think about it.")
6. Assume the child has needs when he acts inappropriately.

Work With What They Give You

In the early days of attachment therapy, when it was known as Rage Reduction Therapy, the treatment was obviously centered around the child's rage. Other feelings were secondary to that end and were often discounted as a result. Some therapists believed that behind all psychopathology was a rage-filled child; if we could lift the rage from her, the pathologies would also dissipate.

At HPI, our experience with rage-filled children supports the premise that intense work focused on the child's rage is needed. But we also recognize and honor the vast variety of feelings that accompanies each of these children. We believe that everything he has to offer – including resistance – is valuable and must be worked with. Thus, our principle of "Work with what they give you" means that we want to work with his sad, mad, scared, happy feelings and whatever else – *including* his resistance. Within the context of high confrontation and high support, if resistance is what he gives us, that is what we will confront and present back to him to be examined. We may not accept the defeating behavior, but *we will work with the feelings that caused it.*

RULE:
For every door you close, you must open a window

For example, given a particular scenario that involves a boy having aggressively tripped his sister, the adult might say something like, "Wow, it looks like you are really struggling (by tripping his sister) with something. There must be something really big going on for you right now. It's not okay for you to act that way, but we can work with whatever is going on. So let's both sit here (or, "You can sit here, because I am busy right now") and process what's going on." This is the crux of treatment:

confront the old ways that don't work, and offer new ways for him to protect himself and to deal with the world.

This approach of working with what is given also necessitates another contract that we get from the child: to "explore for truth." Usually, if this is done in a safe, non-blaming manner, she is receptive to this process. At our treatment center, we train the parents of the children who come to us that one of their main duties is to help their child make the connection with what is going on inside of her that motivates such defeating *outward* behaviors.

What is it that they mostly give us? By definition of the attachment disorder itself, the kids we treat all suffer from:

1. unresolved early life trauma.
2. grief-and-loss issues around that trauma.
3. varying degrees of resistance (through the defense structure).
4. lack of skills to express feelings and get needs met.
5. A broken heart – that is, a damaged core or a core that is largely unknown to them.

Much of the difficulty that we see in foster and adoptive families occurs when the traumatic experiences with the birth situation or later abuse, neglect, or abandonment are transferred by the child from the original sources of the trauma onto the adoptive or foster parents (especially Mom, the primary caregiver).

Much of the work done in the velvet box is to help the child sort out what difficulties she feels right at that moment. She must learn that what belongs to the adoptive or foster parent and what belongs to the birth parents may *not* be the same – *and* how to tell the difference.

This is the point where we confront the whole compound difficulty of the idealization of the birth parents. One hundred percent of all the adoptive children that I have ever worked with have the fantasy that they are going to be reunited with their birth parents and that they will live happily ever after.

There is also the idealization of the aggressor. In this type of situation, the child works harder to please the person who abuses him because that person challenges his very sense of okayness. If he can win that person's love, attention and affection, then he can feel okay. If he does not win that person's love, he cannot feel okay. We try to "cut the transference" and appropriate the correct feeling for each parent: birth, foster, or adoptive.

The central theme of what the kids bring us is *conflict*. They constantly fight this battle of dealing with inner conflict while trying to maintain their outward behavior. Since most of our kids can't always manage this struggle, they bring us their "acting out" behavior. Acting out what? They act out their inner conflict. Their behavior may look random and without purpose, but, as professionals trained to intervene on behalf of the troubled child, we need to look at the inner conflict that drives it.

As we explore for truth with the child, we encourage her to express the *feelings* that go with the events she describes. We, of course, accept the feelings and hold her accountable for her behaviors. "I want to be here with you, but I also want to be with my birth parents," is a common conflict expressed (one way or another) to us by these kids. By accepting her feelings and by encouraging *both* truths to be expressed, her inner conflict begins to be addressed.

RULE:
The way out of conflict is to illuminate both sides.

This technique brings the nature of the child's conflict into her conscious awareness. She is allowed – and encouraged – to express both sides safely, without our disagreement. She gets to experience us as supportive partners, which gives her permission to continue to "act it out" in healthy, verbal ways instead of through the previous defeating behaviors.

According to the teachings at Forest Heights Lodge in Evergreen, Colorado, where I did my internship, this process of helping the child learn to deal appropriately with his feelings usually involves four basic steps:

1. Permission: "Its okay to be mad, sad, etc., but it's *not* okay to behave that way."
2. Modeling: Being honest with your own feelings and discussing them appropriately helps the child put his own feelings into words.
3. Support: Acknowledge the appropriateness of the child's feeling: "It's okay that you hate to clean your room."
4. Push: Identify areas where the child is not expressing feelings overtly. "I think you are mad about cleaning your room. Instead of telling me, you keep forgetting. It's okay to not like it. I want you to look at me and tell me you don't like it."

And finally, remember that they are finished when *they* are finished. We must honor their pace and work with it. Also, they are not necessarily finished simply because they announce that they are. Often, they want to end the processing session prematurely because it is much easier to end than to get into difficult feelings and issues and work through them.

When the child is struggling, resisting, or generally in a "bad" place emotionally, it's time to go to the next attachment principle.

It's All About Distance

In the velvet box, the primary issue is about the distance the child may have from her partner. In order to gain distance from the caregiver (this distance can be as tight as going to the bathroom to as loose as going to the school dance), she is required to be in a "good space" emotionally.

Children without attachment problems feel badly when their unacceptable behavior distances them from their families, and they usually work hard to regain the closeness. They show remorse and a certain demeanor of humility and perhaps sorrowfulness that allows them to regain the favor of their parents and to be close again.

Typically, attachment-disrupted children's primary strategy is to push people away as a defense to being hurt by people they trust. Yet, they know they need the caregiving, so they are once again in conflict. They get what they think they want, which is distance from the adults. The truth is, that's exactly what they *don't* want.

We reverse their typical pushing-away behavior so that it does not provide what they think they want. We insist that they be close to us when they have difficulties and allow them to distance from us when most things are running smoothly for them. In other words, if things are going well for a child and he suddenly makes some bad choices and goes downhill behaviorally, we exercise the principle called "reeling them in." Within the box, as we see a child struggle with tasks she has previously had success with (taking her books to her room, for example), we bring her closer to us and begin the processing and exploring for truth described earlier.

RULE:
The better the child does, the more distance from you he is permitted to have. The more he struggles, the closer he must be to you.

As the adult partner begins to reel the child in, the adult makes proper interventions to help him "get back on track." The adult should be prepared with a series of interventions that gradually bring him closer. One example would be an effective teacher who initially uses words to stop unwanted talking from two students in the back of the room. Next, she might give them "the look" to intervene. Then, perhaps, she would walk to their seats and stand close to them, and, at some point, she might move their seats apart, have them stay after class, do extra work, etc.

When intervening, *the adult should employ the most minimal techniques possible to achieve the desired results.* In other words, use the tool of least resistance to help the child get back on track. We don't need to use our biggest, baddest tools to intervene – just enough intervention to get the job done. Suggestions for steps to take might be:

1. One-to-one: "You are having a hard time this morning. I want you to stay with me so I can help you with that."
2. Sitting: Use sitting for short periods of time (3-5 minutes) to give the child a chance to change rhythms, process feelings, de-escalate behavior.

3. Privilege Restrictions: The restriction should be related to the problem and be set for a brief, specific period of time.

Remember to use natural consequences. Allowing children to suffer or enjoy the logical consequences of life (within reason) is an effective way to teach and discipline them. The use of natural or logical consequences leads to effective cause-and-effect thinking. For example:

If you don't wear your coat,	*then* you will get cold.
If you waste your money,	*then* you won't have money when you need it.
If you hurt your friends,	*then* you won't have friends
If you do not study,	*then* you will not get good grades.

Using natural consequences means that you allow the child to do what he chooses and deal with whatever happens – without your interference either in what he chooses *or* the results.

The point is that, at each intervention, she has a choice to either "get back on track" or continue the disruption. As the disruption continues, so does the reeling in – and the velvet box continues to shrink (her freedom is restricted more and more) until her entire world eventually comes to a screeching halt. There are no more choices until we process the problem and get back on track.

Their World Stops When...

There must be clear consequences when the child does not to respond to the series of interventions by the adult partner. This means that the disruptive behavior has continued (even escalated) despite the adult's attempts at de-escalation. The adult has the ability to stop the child's world (e.g., he does not go to lunch, he does not go to school, he does not go to bed, etc.) until he can work through the conflicting feelings and take care of what was interrupted in his life.

As the adult partners, we have the obligation to shrink the child's world, to shrink the box down to the appropriate size so that she may function optimally, given her emotional difficulty. If she is feeling and acting like a 2-year-old, then modify the box for age 2 functioning. An example would be if a 10-year-old was so angry about being restricted from going roller blading with friends that he refused to drink his orange juice. Now, most 2-year-olds can drink their orange juice, which says, "This 10-year-old is letting his feelings turn him into a 2-year-old." A good parent would never let a 2-year-old go roller blading without supervision. We call this technique "treat-as-age-appropriate."

Clearly, there are many control issues involved when partnering with these children who fear that if they are controlled, they will ultimately kill or be killed.

Using Control to Nurture[1]

If the child is to ever understand and trust that control can actually be supportive and nurturing, the adult must consistently exhibit that belief whenever control, containment, or confrontation are needed to help her get back on track. It is the adult's responsibility to define control as supportive and nurturing and to reinforce that the partnership is for the child's benefit. The challenge is to provide *enough* containment but not stifle her ability to make choices and grow. Following are some principles to help accomplish this.

1. State firmly, "I will take care of you."
2. State that what is best for the child is what you want for him.
3. Prove that you can and will control her when she is not acting to her benefit (by shrinking her velvet box).
4. Use "I" messages and active listening. The use of "I" messages minimizes blaming, allows a choice, and helps the child see that his actions affect others. Active listening gives him the message that his thoughts and ideas are important and serves as a statement of faith in his ability to do problem-solving.
5. Never choose to control issues that you cannot win. For example, never try to control food or toileting issues.
6. Make sure you know who has the problem at any given moment.
7. When the child is out of control, the objective is to assist her as she gains insight into her feelings and control over her behavior.
8. Develop strategies that control the distance the child has from you. Remember that the greater the problem behavior, the closer he needs to be with you.
9. It is absolutely essential to follow the imperative, "for every unit of confrontation, provide an equal unit of support." The support needs to be nurtur-

ing, warm, and close with the partner so that the partnership itself is the reinforcer. Being close *should* feel good.

Chapter 15

Tools to Implement the Attachment Principles

Provide the Tools

The tools of discipline are principles that are developed within the sense of self-awareness as we struggle through life's passages. Through a wide variety of scenarios, life brings forth from within us a sense of "correctness" or "validation" that certain ways of living are more effective than others in the fulfillment of our human potential or to bring us to the end of life's journey as complete as possible.

All religions – and most philosophies – stress that leading a "right" or "disciplined" life is essential to bringing us closer to God and the fulfillment our human nature. The questions of, "What are these tools?" and "How are they developed within us?" are pressing and pertinent.

In *The Road Less Traveled,* M. Scott Peck describes discipline as "…the basic set of tools we require to solve life's problems. Without discipline we can solve nothing. With only some discipline we can solve only some problems. With total discipline we can solve all problems."[1]

Peck continues: "These tools are means by which we experience the pain of problems in such a way as to work them through and solve them successfully, learning and growing in the process. When we teach ourselves and our children discipline, we are teaching them and ourselves how to suffer and also how to grow."[2]

What are these tools, these techniques of experiencing the pain of life's problems constructively? Peck describes the first four[3] (with my interpretation); three more are added for consideration from *The Partnership Model of Discipline*.

1. Delaying of gratification:
   In Freudian terms, the impulsiveness of the id is being engaged by the reality of the ego. In lay terms, it's the lesson Grandma tried to get you to learn: work first, play later; eat dessert last. It is painful to not always get what we want when we want it. The ability to delay gratification develops as the self becomes aware that we are not going to die if we don't receive immediate gratification. As we develop this tool, we are more able to realize the truth about our needs and the urgency of meeting them.

Application to the Partnership Model:
So often, youth, by nature – and especially wounded youth, as described by the results of broken partnerships (attachment disruptions) – haven't yet gained the awareness that they won't die (or that they can even be okay) if most of their needs aren't met immediately. They work hard to avoid the pain of experiencing repeated failure in getting their needs met. As a result, they constantly manipulate their environment and act much like the rat in the Skinner Box that doesn't know when his next gratification will come.

2. Acceptance of responsibility:
   The avoidance of responsibility – primarily by denial and projection – saves people from the painful scrutiny of the perfectionistic demands of the superego – society's pressure. Again, the development of this tool can only occur as the self develops enough strength to

withstand the real or implied threat of criticism, punishment, rejection, or even abandonment.

Application to the model:
Children with histories of broken partnerships simply work harder to avoid the pain that they believe will result if they accept responsibility. They have been wounded by broken or impaired partnership agreements and lack sufficient ego strength to "put it on the line" and risk the pain of criticism, punishment, rejection, or abandonment. It's less painful to deny the problem or to blame others when things go wrong.

3. Dedication to the truth:
   If we are to live our lives with integrity, we must be honest as we face ourselves and the world. Hiding from the embarrassment and pain of who we are only prolongs our living outside the truth. We cannot know our true worth if we cannot accept feedback coming from the people we are supposed to trust. Disciplining ourselves to deal in truth sets us free to be gentle, accepting, and compassionate toward ourselves and others.

Application to the model:
Kids who experience difficulties have already distorted the feedback as to their value and worth. This distortion of self interferes with the process of trusting self and others to the point that they are unable to interact with honesty and integrity. These children typically defend from this risk by rejecting anything that is incongruent with their distorted self-image. They are so invested in defending themselves in rigid ways that they can't emotionally afford the time and energy to gain insight into the truth.

4. Balance:
   As we gain understanding of the components of who we are as human beings, we begin to appreciate the physical, social, intellectual, emotional, and spiritual aspects of ourselves. We develop a sense of our strengths/weaknesses and our joys/disappointments in these areas along with the awareness of what is good or not good for us as we integrate these components into a workable, effective balance.

Application to the model:
Children with difficulties live by very simple rules: they do what works for them, constantly investing their emotional energy into the most likely source of gratification – the path of least resistance. They can't afford the risk of trying new activities, let alone trying to integrate their full range of human functioning. They are out of balance and locked into rigid, limited ways of being.

5. Openness to Learn:
   Developing this tool is an invitation to engage the pain of the truth about self and others. This tool depicts an attitude of care that leads to being open and, therefore, able to "learn the lesson." We simply cannot act in caring ways if we are closed and protected. We cannot be open to learning *and* closed and protected at the same time. If we are open to learning, we are open to risking practicing the other tools of discipline.

Application to the model:
Children who have histories of unmet needs, trauma, rejection, abuse, etc., come to us closed and defended. They cannot take risks, and they tend to remain rigid in their thinking. Learning, for them, is not only difficult because of their intense emotional baggage, but resisted

because of the risk of deviating from what works for them – rigid thinking and protective behaviors.

6. Utilization of Support
   Utilizing support is the crucial first step in the process of developing authentic, lasting relationships. This tool provides the child with the permission and necessary skills to accept the gifts from caregivers. Later, the caregiver will require the reciprocal response from him. He will gradually develop the ability to "form community" and participate successfully in it.

Application to the Partnership Model:
   So often, the attachment-disrupted children we work with come to us with the "self-parenting" attitude already in place. This prevents them from accepting support. Our support can't always ease their pain or solve their problems, but it does provide a safe adult partner to share with – which at least opens the door to partnership and offers them choices. As they exercise these choices, they realize that they don't have to fight their life battles alone.

7. Surrendering:
   We can't have everything, and we can't control everything. Developing this tool brings us to the realization that we are no bigger or smaller than what we really are. As we struggle through life's passages, it is crucial to know when enough is enough. Surrendering seems to contradict directives we are taught, such as, "Fight through it," "Be all you can be," and "Look out for number one."
   Surrendering is not a contradiction but a paradox. It takes a developed self who has fought through it, was all he could be, and looked out for number one, to come all the way to the end of a passage (including life

itself) and just let go and surrender – move past pain and joy and into the upcoming passage.

Application to the model:
Kids who suffer through attachment disruptions tend to hold onto anything that works, including hoarding food, manipulating for attention, and maintaining inflexible behavior patterns. These work because these behaviors give her what she thinks she wants – control over her world, as in, "I'm not surrendering nothin'!" Surrendering would be like asking her to stop her efforts to survive. It would provoke the "kill-or-be-killed" feelings that she works so hard to keep down. The concept of surrendering is advanced and is frighteningly alienating to someone who feels life is literally a struggle for survival.

Teach the Tools of Discipline

Adult partners who work with attachment-disordered children want those kids to be able to learn the tools of discipline and use them effectively in their lives. If this is our hope and our expectation, then it is our responsibility to teach them patiently, compassionately, and well. Learning is the result of both a didactic procedure and the internalization of modeled behavior. Again, there are two methods of teaching these tools:

1. Talk the talk: Use direct dialogue on a cognitive level about the tools: use the language of the tools, process the concepts, and discuss the applications.

2. Walk the walk: Model your behavior for the child so he can internalize the demonstrated attitudes, values, and beliefs for himself.

Create Gifts to Accompany the Tools of Discipline

So often, the adults who work with children have wonderful standards of performance, proper expectations of effort and outcomes for them – but they are rarely charged with or held accountable for the contributions they offer the child in partnership. This partnership model offers an enhancement to the learning of these tools – gifts the adult can give the child to facilitate her learning, partnering, and passage. The adult must highly value the intention of creating gifts for the child in specific circumstances as they partner.

Adults would do well to constantly ask themselves, "As I see this child struggling, what gift can I offer him that enhances his chances of success? How can I help my partner without enabling or getting hooked into his issues?"

For the tool of...	Give the gift of...
1. Delay of gratification	Trust: This is the gift you must give if you are asking a child to postpone a particular negative behavior so that a better one can be worked out later.
2. Acceptance of responsibility	Safety: This is the gift you must give if you are asking a child to be honest about and own her behaviors.

3. Dedication to
   the truth

   Insight:
   Your own dedication to the truth can help to develop his so he can realize the truth and the consequences of living it.

4. Balance

   Practice:
   Free, no-strings-attached chances to experiment with what works best for her and the partnership.

5. Openness to learn

   Caring:
   This is what we model as we process his struggles through the passage.

6. Utilization of support

   Availability:
   Be there physically and emotionally. Be attentive and engaged when interacting so she experiences your full presence.

7. Surrendering

   Compassion:
   This is the gift we must give if we ask him to deal with losses and get on with life.

Epilogue

It's the middle of July, and I'm sitting in my office suffering though a heat wave. Normally, I wouldn't give two thoughts to the air-conditioning, but today it reminds me of Donald and his successful journey into adulthood.

Today, he is gainfully employed fixing air-conditioning and heating. He completed his Associate's Degree, and he is planning to get married. Quite a turnaround from the angry kid I met who wanted to kill the "punk" who took his stuff, who wanted to strangle the world.

Donald's journey was a true partnership of family, friends and professionals – a testament to strength, courage, and the hope that The Love Disorder can be healed. As the years of the odometer click us into the new millennium, I hear a lot of talk about the "end times," about how bad things have become. I even know people who think the end is here and ask, "Why bother?"

But I think about the next "Donald" who will be in my office tomorrow. I think about the chance that he needs, the chance his family deserves; I think about the power of the Partnership Model and the hope we must carry into the next century. Love is not meant to be a "disorder."

Notes

Introduction
1. Thomas, Kim. <u>Defended Against Love: Attachment Disorder, its Nature, Etiology and Treatment.</u> Unpublished Manuscript, The Naropa Institute, Boulder, CO: 1998, 7.

Chapter 1
1. Vonnegut, Kurt. <u>Slapstick.</u> New York, NY: Dell Publishing, 1976.
2. Clinton, Hillary Rodham. <u>It Takes a Village: and Other Lessons Children Teach Us.</u> New York, NY: Touchstone Books, 1998
3. Neifert, Marianne. <u>Dr. Mom's Parenting Guide.</u> New York: Penguin Books, 1991, 14.

Chapter 3
1. Egan, Timothy. "Killing Sprees Tied by String of Youth Rage," <u>The Denver Post,</u> June 14, 1998, 1.
2. CASA (1997). <u>Back to School Survey.</u> [cited June 26, 1998], available: http://www.ed.govoffices/OESE
3. "Alcoholism and Drug Abuse Week," February 7, 1994, v6, n6, 2. Available: http://sbweb2.med.iacnet.com
4. Magid, Ken & McKelvey, Carole). <u>High Risk: Children Without a Conscience.</u> Golden, CO: M & M Publishing, 1987, 164.
5. The Jason Foundation (1998). <u>Youth Suicide Fact Sheet.</u> 1997, 1998 [cited June 22, 1998], available: http://www.geocities.com

6. Manciaux, Michael, "Violent youth," World Health 46th Year, No. 1, January-February 1993, 24.
7. ---. 24.
8. Goode, Stephen. "Insight on the News," 11.46 (1995), 14.2, available: http://sbweb3.med.iacnet.com
9. Egan, Timothy. "Killing Sprees Tied by String of Youth Rage," The Denver Post, June 14, 1998, 22.
10. "Each One, Teach One 1998: Selected Research Findings on School Violence," [cited June 23, 1998]: available: http://www.ncsu.edu/cpsb/eoto98.htm
11. Pitts, Leonard. "School Tragedy's Bitter Lesson: Society's Coldness Has Created Kids Who Don't Feel." The Miami Herald, 29 January 1997: 129.
12. Eftimiades, Maria, et al. Why are Kids Killing? People, 23 June 1997: 46–53.
13. ---. 46.
14. Office of National Drug Policy, "Pulse check." Available: http://www.health.org
15. McCarthy, Nora. "Teen Drug Use Rises..." Newsday, 21 August 1996, AO7.
16. Reed, Mack. "Teenage Addiction Escalates, Worries Experts," Los Angeles Times, 22 September 1996, 1
17. Smith, Sandra & Ramirez, Sharon. "Teenage Birth Rates – Variations by State." Public Health Reports, March – April 1997, 112.2: 173
18. Allen-Mills, Tony. "U.S. Agonizes Over Soaring Teen Births." The New York Times, 12 January 1997: 19.
19. ---. 19.
20. Chassler, Sey. "What Teenage Girls Say About Pregnancy." Parade, 2 February 1997: 4.
21. Garfinkel, Irwin & McLanahan, Sara S. Single Mothers and Their Children: A New American Dilemma. Washington, D.C., Urban Institute, 1996: 11.

Chapter 4
1. Toffler, Alvin. <u>Future Shock.</u> Bantam Books, 1991.
2. Magid, Ken & McKelvey, Carole. <u>High Risk: Children Without a Conscience.</u> Golden, CO: M & M Publishing, 1987, 167.
3. Seabach, Linda. "Money Shouldn't Control Policy on Sex Education," <u>Rocky Mountain News,</u> 11 January 1998, 2B.
4. ---. 2B.

Chapter 5
1. Karen, Robert. <u>Becoming Attached: First Relationships and How They Shape Our Capacity to Love.</u> New York: Warner Books, 1994, 93.
2. ---. 94.
3. McKeachie, W. J., & Doyle, C. L. <u>Psychology.</u> USA: Addison Wesley, 78.
4. Karen, Robert. <u>Becoming Attached: First Relationships and How They Shape Our Capacity to Love.</u> New York: Warner Books, 1994, 44.
5. ---. 94–95.
6. ---. 95.
7. ---. 95.
8. McKeachie, W. J., & Doyle, C. L. <u>Psychology.</u> USA: Addison Wesley, 211.
9. Sroufe, Alan L. "Appraisal: Bowlby's Contribution to Psychoanalytic Theory and Developmental Psychology; Attachment: Separation: Loss." Association for Child Psychology and Child Psychiatry, 27.6 (1986): 843.
10. Bowlby, John. "Attachment Theory, Separation Anxiety and Mourning." <u>American Handbook of Psychiatry.</u> New York: Basic Books, 1975: 295.

Chapter 6

1. Fraiberg, Thelma. <u>Every Child's Birthright: In Defense of Mothering.</u> 1979: available: Amazon.com [asino553121472].
2. Rutter, M. <u>Maternal Deprivation Reassessed.</u> New York: Penguin, 1981.
3. Cline, Foster W. <u>Hope for High Risk and Rage Filled Children: Reactive Attachment Disorder Theory and Intrusive Therapy.</u> Evergreen, CO: EC Publications, 1991: 42–45
4. ---. 2
5. ---. 3–4
6. ---. 15
7. ---. 6
8. ---. 5
9. ---. 4

Chapter 7

1. Cline, Foster W. <u>Understanding and Treating the Severely Disturbed Child.</u> Evergreen, CO: EC Publications, 1991: 59

Chapter 8

1. Ainsworth, Mary, et al. <u>Pathways of Attachment,</u> Hillsdale, NJ: Erlbaum, 1978.
2. Rutter, M. "Attachment and the Development of Social Relationships." <u>Scientific Foundations of Developmental Psychiatry.</u> London: Heinemann Medical, 1980.
3. Boeding, Conrad, "An Historical Perspective of Attachment Research," 1 August 1985, 26.
4. Ainsworth, Mary. "Infant–Mother Attachment," <u>American Psychologist,</u> 34, 1979: 932-937.
5. Sroufe, L. A. "Appraisal: Bowlby's Contribution to Psychoanalytic Theory and Developmental Psychology;

Attachment: Separation: Loss. <u>Association for Child Psychology and Child Psychiatry,</u> 27.6, 1986: 846.
6. Ainsworth, Mary, et al. <u>Pathways of Attachment,</u> Hillsdale, NJ: Erlbaum, 1978: 932–937.
7. Robertson, J. & Robertson, T. "Young Children in Brief Separation: A Fresh Look. <u>Psychoanalytic Study of the Child,</u> 26, 1971: 264-315.
8. Kirgan, D., et al. <u>Attachment Impairment.</u> Unpublished monograph. San Rafael, CA., 1982.

Section Three
1. Adams, Bryan, Lange, & R. J., Komen, M. <u>(Everything I Do) I Do it for You.</u> Produced: Adams, Bryan & Lange, R. J. Performed: Adams, Bryan. A & M Records, Inc. 1991.

Chapter 9
1. Horney, Karen. <u>The Person: An Introduction to Personality Psychology.</u> San Diego, CA: Harcourt Brace & Company, 1994: 90–92.
2. ---. 90–92.
3. ---. 90–92.
4. ---. 90–92.
5. Allen, W. <u>Synopsis and Nosology: Being an Arrangement and Definition of Diseases,</u> Hartford, CT: Edward Gray. New York: Ready microprint, 1793, 1985, N. 25360.
6. Goldeson, Robert M. <u>The Encyclopedia of Human Behavior.</u> Garden City, NY: Doubleday & Co., Inc., 1970: 1063.
7. ---. 941.
8. <u>American Psychological Association, Diagnostic and Statistical Manual of Mental Disorders, Fourth Edition.</u> Washington, DC: American Psychiatric Association, 1994.

9. Peck, M. Scott. The Road Less Traveled. New York: Simon & Schuster, Inc., 1978: 35.
10. ---. 36.
11. ---. 38.
12. ---. 36.

Chapter 10
1. Sroufe, L. Alan. "Appraisal: Bowlby's Contribution to Psychoanalytic Theory and Developmental Psychology; Attachment: Separation: Loss." Association for Child Psychology and Child Psychiatry, 27.6, 1986: 841-849.
2. Gerald, Cory. Theory and Practice of Counseling Psychology, 4th Edition. Pacific Grove, CA: Brosky Cole, 1991.

Chapter 11
1. Gibran, Kahlil. The Prophet. New York: Alfred A. Knopf, 1997: 17.

Chapter 12
1. American Psychological Association, Diagnostic and Statistical Manual of Mental Disorders, Fourth Edition. Washington, DC: American Psychiatric Association, 1994.
2. Andreas, S. & Faulkner, C. NLP: the New Technology of Achievement. New York: William Morrow & Co., 1994.

Chapter 14
1. Curtis, Ray. "Control as Nurture," Unpublished Manuscript, Forest Heights Lodge, Evergreen, CO: 1986.

Chapter 15
1. Peck, M. Scott. <u>The Road Less Traveled.</u> New York: Simon & Schuster, Inc., 1978: 15–16.
2. ---. 18.
3. ---. 18.
4. Boeding, Conrad, <u>The Partnership Model of Discipline.</u> Lakewood, CO: Human Passages Institute, 1997: 16–19.